Better Homes and Gardens®
pizzas
COOKING FOR TODAY

BETTER HOMES AND GARDENS® BOOKS
Des Moines

BETTER HOMES AND GARDENS® BOOKS
An Imprint of Meredith® Books
President, Book Group: Joseph J. Ward
Vice President and Editorial Director: Elizabeth P. Rice
Executive Editor: Nancy N. Green
Managing Editor: Christopher Cavanaugh
Art Director: Ernest Shelton
Test Kitchen Director: Sharon Stilwell

PIZZAS
Editor: Mary Major Williams
Writer: Linda Henry
Associate Art Director: Tom Wegner
Graphic Production Coordinator: Paula Forest
Production Manager: Doug Johnston
Test Kitchen Product Supervisor: Marilyn Cornelius
Food Stylists: Lynn Blanchard, Janet Pittman, Jennifer Peterson
Photographers: Mike Dieter, Scott Little
Cover Photographer: Andy Lyons

On the cover: Whole Wheat Pizza Tart (see recipe, page 105)

Meredith Corporation Corporate Officers:
Chairman of the Executive Committee: E. T. Meredith III
Chairman of the Board, President and Chief Executive Officer: Jack D. Rehm
Group Presidents: Joseph J. Ward, Books; William T. Kerr, Magazines; Philip A. Jones, Broadcasting;
    Allen L. Sabbag, Real Estate
Vice Presidents: Leo R. Armatis, Corporate Relations; Thomas G. Fisher, General Counsel and Secretary;
    Larry D. Hartsook, Finance; Michael A. Sell, Treasurer; Kathleen J. Zehr, Controller and Assistant Secretary

WE CARE!

All of us at Better Homes and Gardens® Books are dedicated to providing you with the information
and ideas you need to create tasty foods. We welcome your comments and suggestions. Write us at:
Better Homes and Gardens® Books, Cookbook Editorial Department, 1716 Locust St., Des Moines,
IA 50309-3023

Our seal assures you that every recipe in *Pizzas* has been
tested in the Better Homes and Gardens® Test Kitchen.
This means that each recipe is practical and reliable, and
meets our high standards of taste appeal. We guarantee
your satisfaction with this book for as long as you own it.

Pizza—one of America's favorite foods—is as much fun to make as it is to eat! The 65 plus recipes we've included here are positive proof of that.

In this book you will find pizza recipes with traditional toppers such as pepperoni, hamburger, sausage, and mozzarella cheese. Other recipes offer more exotic toppings such as shiitake mushrooms, artichoke hearts, pesto, smoked salmon, shrimp, and feta cheese. Additional recipes call for familiar pizza ingredients in the form of a casserole, bread, burger, or turnover. And for your sweet tooth, we've included dessert pizzas made with brownie and cookie crusts and topped with fruit and candy.

As every pizza connoisseur knows, the secret to a great pizza is the crust. And since preferences range from thin and crispy to thick and breadlike, we've offered you a wide variety of choices. You can make your own or start with frozen bread dough or hot roll mix. You can also use refrigerated pizza dough or Italian bread shells.

So how about pizza tonight? Serve up Bacon-Cheeseburger Pizza, California-Style Chicken Pizza, or Pizza Burgers. Once you've made your own pizza, you'll turn to these recipes again and again.

CONTENTS

PIZZA DOUGH

- 2¾ to 3¼ cups all-purpose flour
- 1 package active dry yeast
- ¼ teaspoon salt
- 1 cup warm water (120° to 130°)
- 2 tablespoons cooking oil

In a large bowl combine *1¼ cups* of the flour, the yeast, and the salt. Add warm water and oil. Beat with an electric mixer on low speed for 30 seconds, scraping bowl constantly. Beat on high speed for 3 minutes. Using a spoon, stir in as much of the remaining flour as you can. Turn dough out onto a lightly floured surface. Knead in enough remaining flour to make a moderately stiff dough that is smooth and elastic (6 to 8 minutes total). Divide dough in half. Cover and let rest 10 minutes.

Roll out, add toppings, and bake as directed in the individual recipes.

Nutrition information per serving (⅙ recipe): 236 calories, 6 g protein, 41 g carbohydrate, 5 g fat (1 g saturated), 0 mg cholesterol, 91 mg sodium, 80 mg potassium.

Whole Wheat Pizza Dough: Prepare Pizza Dough as above, except reduce all-purpose flour to 1¾ to 2¼ cups; add 1 cup *whole wheat flour* after beating.

Nutrition information per serving (⅙ recipe): 234 calories, 7 g protein, 41 g carbohydrate, 5 g fat (1 g saturated), 0 mg cholesterol, 92 mg sodium, 140 mg potassium.

Cornmeal Pizza Dough: Prepare Pizza Dough as above, except reduce all-purpose flour to 2 to 2½ cups and add ¾ cup *yellow cornmeal* after beating.

Nutrition information per serving (⅙ recipe): 246 calories, 6 g protein, 43 g carbohydrate, 5 g fat (1 g saturated), 0 mg cholesterol, 91 mg sodium, 93 mg potassium.

Cheese Pizza Dough: Prepare Pizza Dough as above, except add ½ cup grated *Parmesan cheese* with the yeast.

Nutrition information per serving (⅙ recipe): 274 calories, 9 g protein, 41 g carbohydrate, 8 g fat (2 g saturated), 7 mg cholesterol, 246 mg sodium, 89 mg potassium.

Garlic and Herb Pizza Dough: Prepare Pizza Dough as above, except add 2 teaspoons dried *basil, oregano, or Italian seasoning,* crushed, and 1 clove *garlic,* minced, with the dry ingredients.

Nutrition information per serving (⅙ recipe): 237 calories, 6 g protein, 41 g carbohydrate, 5 g fat (1 g saturated), 0 mg cholesterol, 91 mg sodium, 90 mg potassium.

HERBED PIZZA SAUCE

¾ cup chopped onion
2 cloves garlic, minced
1 tablespoon olive oil, margarine, or butter
1 14½-ounce can tomatoes, cut up
1 8-ounce can tomato sauce
1 bay leaf
1 tablespoon snipped fresh basil or 1 teaspoon dried basil, crushed
1 tablespoon snipped fresh oregano or 1 teaspoon dried oregano, crushed
1 teaspoon fennel seed, crushed (optional)
½ teaspoon sugar
¼ teaspoon pepper

Cook onion and garlic in oil. Stir in remaining ingredients. Bring to boiling. Reduce heat; simmer, uncovered, for 35 to 40 minutes or to desired consistency, stirring occasionally. Discard bay leaf. Makes 1¾ cups (enough for 2 pizzas or 6 servings).

Nutrition information per serving: 60 calories, 2 g protein, 10 g carbohydrate, 3 g fat (0 g saturated), 0 mg cholesterol, 341 mg sodium, 342 mg potassium.

Hot and Spicy Pizza Sauce: Prepare as above except reduce the chopped onion to ½ cup and add ½ cup chopped green pepper with onion. Omit bay leaf; add ⅛ to ¼ teaspoon *ground red pepper* and ⅛ teaspoon *chili powder* with the remaining ingredients.

Nutrition information per serving: 62 calories, 2 g protein, 10 g carbohydrate, 3 g fat (0 g saturated), 0 mg cholesterol, 431 mg sodium, 358 mg potassium.

PARMESAN PIZZA SAUCE

⅓ cup finely chopped onion
2 cloves garlic, minced
1 tablespoon margarine or butter
1 tablespoon all-purpose flour
⅛ teaspoon white pepper
1 cup milk
¼ teaspoon instant chicken bouillon granules
¼ cup grated Parmesan cheese

In a small saucepan cook the onion and garlic in margarine or butter till onion is tender but not brown. Stir in the flour and pepper. Add the milk and bouillon granules all at once. Cook and stir till slightly thickened and bubbly. Stir in the Parmesan cheese. Makes about 1 cup sauce (enough for 1 pizza or 3 servings).

Nutrition information per serving: 133 calories, 7 g protein, 9 g carbohydrate, 8 g fat (3 g saturated), 13 mg cholesterol, 313 mg sodium, 179 g potassium.

SOUTHWESTERN STUFFED PIZZA

For a doubly delicious taste, this robust pizza packs a zesty meat and corn filling between two crusts.

1½ pounds ground beef
1   12-ounce jar salsa
1   8-ounce can whole kernel corn, drained
1½ cups shredded cheddar cheese (6 ounces)
½   cup sliced pitted ripe olives
2   to 3 tablespoons snipped fresh cilantro
¾   teaspoon ground cumin
¼   teaspoon pepper
1   16-ounce package hot roll mix
¼   cup cornmeal
½   teaspoon ground cumin
1   beaten egg

For filling, in a large skillet cook ground beef till brown. Drain fat. Stir in salsa, corn, cheese, olives, cilantro, the ¾ teaspoon cumin, and pepper. Set aside.

Prepare hot roll mix according to package directions, except stir the cornmeal and the ½ teaspoon cumin into the flour mixture and increase hot tap water to 1¼ cups. Turn dough out onto a lightly floured surface. Knead about 5 minutes or till smooth and elastic. Divide dough in half. Cover and let rest 5 minutes.

Meanwhile, grease an 11- to 13-inch pizza pan. Sprinkle with additional cornmeal, if desired. On a lightly floured surface, roll each half of dough into a circle 1 inch larger than pizza pan. Transfer one crust to pan. Spread meat mixture over dough.

Cut several slits in remaining crust. Place top crust on meat mixture. Trim and flute edges. Brush with beaten egg; sprinkle with additional cornmeal, if desired.

Bake in a 375° oven for 30 to 35 minutes or till pastry is golden and pizza is heated through. If necessary to prevent overbrowning, cover pizza with foil after 20 minutes. Makes 6 servings.

Nutrition information per serving: 724 calories, 42 g protein, 69 g carbohydrate, 31 g fat (12 g saturated), 171 mg cholesterol, 1,305 mg sodium, 589 mg potassium.

BACON-CHEESEBURGER PIZZA

If burgers are a popular item in your house, then this meaty pizza will be a surefire hit.

Pizza Dough (see recipe, page 4)
1 **pound ground beef**
1 **cup chopped onion**
   Herbed Pizza Sauce (see recipe, page 5) or one 15-ounce can or one 15½-ounce jar pizza sauce
2 **medium tomatoes, very thinly sliced**
6 **slices bacon, cut into 2-inch pieces, crisp-cooked, and drained**
3 **cups shredded cheddar, American, or Cojack cheese (12 ounces)**

Prepare Pizza Dough. Grease two 11- to 13-inch pizza pans or baking sheets. On a lightly floured surface, roll each half of dough into a circle 1 inch larger than pizza pan. Transfer dough to pans. Build up edges slightly. Prick generously with a fork. Do not let rise. Bake in a 425° oven for 10 to 12 minutes or till lightly browned.

Meanwhile, in a large skillet cook ground beef and onion till meat is brown and onion is tender. Drain fat. Spread pizza sauce over hot crusts. Sprinkle with ground beef mixture. Top with tomato slices and bacon pieces. Sprinkle with cheese. Bake about 12 minutes more or till cheese melts and sauce is bubbly. Makes 8 servings.

Nutrition information per serving: 543 calories, 29 g protein, 42 g carbohydrate, 29 g fat (13 g saturated), 84 mg cholesterol, 697 mg sodium, 618 mg potassium.

DEEP-DISH PIZZA

This substantial, two-crust pizza first became popular in Chicago back in the early 1940's.

1   16-ounce package hot roll mix
1   pound ground beef
1   cup chopped onion
2   cloves garlic, minced
1   cup Herbed Pizza Sauce
     (see recipe, page 5) or one 8-ounce
     can pizza sauce
1   7-ounce jar roasted red sweet peppers,
     drained and chopped
1   4-ounce can sliced mushrooms,
     drained
1½ cups shredded provolone cheese
     (6 ounces)
1   10-ounce package frozen chopped
     spinach, thawed and well drained
1   slightly beaten egg

Prepare hot roll mix according to package directions through the kneading step. Cover; let rest.

Meanwhile, in a large skillet cook ground beef, onion, and garlic till meat is brown and onion is tender. Drain fat. Stir in pizza sauce, red sweet peppers, and mushrooms. Cook till heated through. Cover and keep warm.

Grease the bottom of a 9-inch springform pan. On a lightly floured surface roll *three-fourths* of the dough into a 13-inch circle. Fit into the bottom and press up the sides of the springform pan. Sprinkle bottom of dough with *½ cup* of the provolone cheese. Spoon meat mixture over cheese.

Pat spinach dry with paper towels. Combine spinach, egg, and remaining provolone cheese. Spread spinach mixture over meat mixture. Roll remaining dough into a 9-inch circle; place atop spinach mixture. Fold excess bottom dough under; pinch to seal.

Bake in a 350° oven for 40 to 45 minutes or till golden brown. Cool 10 minutes on a wire rack. To serve, remove sides of springform pan; cut into wedges. Makes 8 servings.

Nutrition information per serving: 480 calories, 27 g protein, 53 g carbohydrate, 18 g fat (7 g saturated), 102 mg cholesterol, 804 mg sodium, 581 mg potassium.

HEARTY MEAT PIZZA

Ground beef, pepperoni, and Canadian-style bacon top this scrumptious, stick-to-the-ribs pizza.

Pizza Dough (see recipe, page 4)
½ **pound ground beef and/or bulk Italian sausage or pork sausage**
1 **cup chopped onion**
Herbed Pizza Sauce (see recipe, page 5) or one 15-ounce can or one 15½-ounce jar pizza sauce
1 **3½-ounce package sliced pepperoni**
1 **cup cut-up Canadian-style bacon**
1 **cup chopped green pepper**
2 **cups shredded mozzarella cheese (8 ounces)**
¼ **cup grated Parmesan or Romano cheese**

Prepare Pizza Dough. Grease two 11- to 13-inch pizza pans or baking sheets. On a lightly floured surface, roll each half of dough into a circle 1 inch larger than pizza pan. Transfer to pans. Build up edges slightly. Flute edges, if desired. Prick dough generously with a fork. Do not let rise. Bake in a 425° oven for 10 to 12 minutes or till lightly browned.

Meanwhile, in a large skillet cook ground beef and/or sausage and onion till meat is brown and onion is tender. Drain fat. Spread pizza sauce over hot crusts. Sprinkle with beef mixture. Top with pepperoni, Canadian-style bacon, and green pepper. Sprinkle with mozzarella and Parmesan or Romano cheese.

Bake for 10 to 12 minutes more or till cheese melts and sauce is bubbly. Makes 6 to 8 servings.

Nutrition information per serving: 699 calories, 42 g protein, 57 g carbohydrate, 33 g fat (13 g saturated), 98 mg cholesterol, 1,427 mg sodium, 870 mg potassium.

EASY TACO PIZZA

This hearty south-of-the border pizza is popular with both kids and adults alike.

Cornmeal Pizza Dough
   (see recipe, page 4)
¾ pound ground beef
1 cup chopped onion
1 8-ounce can tomato sauce
1 2¼-ounce can sliced pitted ripe olives, drained
1 1¼-ounce envelope taco seasoning mix
2 cups shredded cheddar cheese (8 ounces)
2 cups shredded lettuce
2 cups chopped tomatoes
2 medium avocados, seeded, peeled, and chopped
1 8-ounce carton dairy sour cream
   Chili powder (optional)

Prepare Cornmeal Pizza Dough. Grease two 11- to 13-inch pizza pans or baking sheets. On a lightly floured surface, roll each half of dough into a circle 1 inch larger than pizza pan. Transfer dough to pans. Build up edges slightly. Flute edges, if desired. Prick generously with a fork. Do not let rise. Bake in a 425° oven for 10 to 12 minutes or till lightly browned.

Meanwhile, in a large skillet cook ground beef and onion till meat is brown and onion is tender. Drain fat. Stir in tomato sauce, olives, and taco seasoning mix; heat through.

Spread ground beef mixture over hot crusts. Sprinkle with cheese. Bake about 12 minutes or till cheese melts. Top with lettuce, tomatoes, and avocados. Spoon sour cream into center of each pizza. Sprinkle sour cream with chili powder, if desired. Makes 6 servings.

Nutrition information per serving: 726 calories, 32 g protein, 56 g carbohydrate, 45 g fat (15 g saturated), 90 mg cholesterol, 1,274 mg sodium, 1,079 mg potassium.

TEX-MEX PIZZA

To make this pizza taste more like a taco, sprinkle it with 2 cups of crushed tortilla chips before serving.

Cornmeal Pizza Dough
  (see recipe, page 4)
1 pound ground beef or bulk chorizo
  Hot and Spicy Pizza Sauce
  (see recipe, page 5)
1 15-ounce can black beans, rinsed and
  drained
½ cup chopped red sweet pepper
3 tablespoons finely chopped jalapeño
  peppers
2 tablespoons snipped fresh cilantro
3 cups shredded Monterey Jack cheese
  (12 ounces)
½ cup salsa

Prepare Cornmeal Pizza Dough. Grease two 11- to 13-inch pizza pans or baking sheets. On a lightly floured surface, roll each half of dough into a circle 1 inch larger than pizza pan. Transfer dough to pans. Build up edges slightly; score edges with a knife, if desired. Prick dough generously with a fork. Do not let rise. Bake in a 425° oven for 10 to 12 minutes or till lightly browned.

Meanwhile, in a large skillet cook ground beef or chorizo till brown. Drain fat. Spread Hot and Spicy Pizza Sauce over hot crusts. Sprinkle with cooked beef or chorizo, black beans, red sweet pepper, jalapeño peppers, and cilantro. Sprinkle with Monterey Jack cheese. Bake about 12 minutes more or till cheese melts and sauce is bubbly. Serve with salsa. Makes 8 servings.

Nutrition information per serving: 539 calories, 30 g protein, 49 g carbohydrate, 26 g fat (12 g saturated), 73 mg cholesterol, 836 mg sodium, 680 mg potassium.

SHEPHERD'S PIZZA

Ground lamb, Italian seasoning, and mozzarella cheese—plus a potato crust woven into a lattice—make this hearty pizza an original.

1 16-ounce package hot roll mix
¼ cup instant mashed potato flakes
1 8-ounce carton plain yogurt
½ cup water
1 egg
1 pound ground lamb or beef
2 cups shredded mozzarella cheese
(8 ounces)
1 cup frozen peas and carrots
1 medium tomato, seeded and coarsely
chopped
¼ cup sliced green onion
1½ teaspoons dried Italian seasoning,
crushed
¼ teaspoon pepper
1 tablespoon milk

In a large mixing bowl combine hot roll mix and potato flakes. In a saucepan heat yogurt and water till warm (120° to 130°). Mixture may appear curdled. Stir yogurt mixture and egg into flour mixture. Turn dough out onto a lightly floured surface. Knead about 5 minutes or till smooth and elastic. Shape dough into a ball. Cover and let rest 5 minutes.

Meanwhile, in a large skillet cook ground lamb or beef till brown. Drain fat. Stir in *1¼ cups* of the cheese, peas and carrots, tomato, green onion, Italian seasoning, and pepper.

Grease an 11- to 13-inch pizza pan. On a lightly floured surface, roll *two-thirds* of the dough into a circle 1 inch larger than pizza pan. Transfer dough to pan. Build up edges slightly. Do not let rise. Spread meat mixture over crust. Sprinkle with remaining cheese.

Roll out remaining dough into a circle that matches the diameter of your pizza pan; cut into ½-inch wide strips. Weave strips over filling to make a lattice-top crust. Trim ends of strips even with edge of pan. Pinch ends of strips to bottom dough to seal. Brush dough with milk.

Bake in a 400° oven for 30 to 35 minutes or till cheese melts and pizza is heated through. If necessary to prevent overbrowning, cover pizza with foil after 20 minutes. Makes 6 servings.

Nutrition information per serving: 604 calories, 35 g protein, 64 g carbohydrate, 22 g fat (10 g saturated), 115 mg cholesterol, 591 mg sodium, 535 mg potassium.

QUICK-AND-EASY BEEF PIZZA

Ready in 15 minutes, this colorful pizza lives up to its name!

1   green pepper, cut into bite-size strips
1   small onion, sliced and separated
        into rings
1   tablespoon olive oil or cooking oil
1   16-ounce package Boboli (12-inch
        Italian bread shell)
6   ounces fully cooked beef, cut into
        thin strips
1   cup cherry tomatoes, halved
1   cup shredded Swiss cheese (4 ounces)
2   tablespoons grated Parmesan cheese

In a large skillet cook green pepper and onion in hot oil till tender. Set aside.

Place bread shell on a lightly greased baking sheet. Top with beef, onion mixture, and cherry tomatoes. Sprinkle with Swiss cheese and Parmesan cheese.

Bake in a 400° oven about 8 minutes or till cheese melts and pizza is heated through. Makes 4 servings.

Nutrition information per serving: 584 calories, 34 g protein, 55 g carbohydrate, 26 g fat (9 g saturated), 67 mg cholesterol, 784 mg sodium, 370 mg potassium.

REUBEN PIZZA

All the ingredients of the ever-popular Reuben sandwich—corned beef, sauerkraut, and Swiss cheese—top this tasty pizza.

1   16-ounce loaf frozen whole wheat
     bread dough, thawed
½   cup Thousand Island salad dressing
2   cups shredded Swiss cheese (8 ounces)
6   ounces thinly sliced cooked corned
     beef
1   8-ounce can sauerkraut, rinsed and
     well drained
½   teaspoon caraway seed
     Dill pickle slices, chopped (optional)

On a lightly floured surface, roll bread dough into a 14-inch circle. Transfer to a greased 13-inch pizza pan. Build up edges slightly. Prick generously with a fork. Bake in a 375° oven for 20 to 25 minutes or till light brown.

Spread *half* of the salad dressing over hot crust. Sprinkle with *half* of the Swiss cheese. Arrange corned beef over cheese. Drizzle remaining salad dressing over corned beef. Top with sauerkraut and remaining Swiss cheese. Sprinkle with caraway seed.

Bake about 10 minutes more or till cheese melts and pizza is heated through. Top with chopped dill pickle, if desired. Makes 6 servings.

Nutrition information per serving: 474 calories, 22 g protein, 38 g carbohydrate, 26 g fat (10 g saturated), 69 mg cholesterol, 724 mg sodium, 220 mg potassium.

PASTA PIZZA
A pasta crust makes this pizza different from all the rest.

2 cups gemelli or corkscrew macaroni
1 slightly beaten egg
¼ cup milk
2 tablespoons grated Parmesan or
    Romano cheese
1 pound ground pork or ground beef
1 cup chopped onion
2 cloves garlic, minced
    Herbed Pizza Sauce (see recipe,
    page 5) or one 15-ounce can or
    one 15½-ounce jar pizza sauce
¼ teaspoon crushed red pepper
1 4-ounce can sliced mushrooms,
    drained
½ cup chopped green pepper
1 cup shredded mozzarella cheese
    (4 ounces)

Cook pasta according to package directions; drain well. Rinse with cold water; drain again. Combine egg, milk, and Parmesan or Romano cheese. Stir in pasta. Spread pasta mixture evenly into a greased 13-inch pizza pan. Bake in a 350° oven for 20 minutes.

Meanwhile, in a large skillet cook ground pork or beef, onion, and garlic till meat is brown and onion is tender. Drain fat. Stir in pizza sauce and crushed red pepper. Bring to boiling. Reduce heat. Cover and simmer for 10 minutes. Spoon meat mixture over baked pasta crust. Top with mushrooms and green pepper. Sprinkle with mozzarella cheese.

Bake for 10 to 12 minutes more or till mozzarella cheese melts and pizza is heated through. Makes 6 servings.

Nutrition information per serving: 331 calories, 21 g protein, 33 g carbohydrate, 13 g fat (3 g saturated), 83 mg cholesterol, 590 mg sodium, 611 mg potassium.

STUFFED PIZZA FLORENTINE

Be sure to squeeze all the moisture out of the spinach so your pizza doesn't get soggy.

Whole Wheat Pizza Dough
   (see recipe, page 4)
1 cup shredded mozzarella cheese
   (4 ounces)
1 10-ounce package frozen chopped
   spinach, thawed and well drained
1 slightly beaten egg
¼ cup grated Parmesan cheese
1 3½-ounce package sliced pepperoni
1 2-ounce can mushroom stems and
   pieces, drained
¼ cup sliced pitted ripe olives (optional)
1 slightly beaten egg
1 tablespoon grated Parmesan cheese

Prepare Whole Wheat Pizza Dough. Grease a 13-inch pizza pan. On a lightly floured surface, roll each half of dough into a 13-inch circle. Transfer one circle to pizza pan. Build up edges slightly. Sprinkle with mozzarella cheese. Set aside.

Pat spinach dry with paper towels. Combine spinach, 1 slightly beaten egg, and the ¼ cup Parmesan cheese. Spread spinach mixture over mozzarella cheese. Top with pepperoni, mushrooms, and, if desired, ripe olives. Brush edge of dough with some of the remaining slightly beaten egg. Top with second circle of dough. Pinch edges to seal. Score edges with a knife, if desired. Cut 14 to 16 slits, about 1 inch long, in top crust for steam to escape. Brush crust with the remaining egg and sprinkle with the 1 tablespoon Parmesan cheese.

Bake in a 375° oven for 30 to 35 minutes or till heated through. Makes 6 servings.

Nutrition information per serving: 436 calories, 20 g protein, 47 g carbohydrate, 19 g fat (7 g saturated), 95 mg cholesterol, 705 mg sodium, 295 mg potassium.

MEXICALI PIZZA

Chorizo (chor EE so) is a hot-and-peppery, coarsely ground, Mexican sausage. Look for it in the meat section at larger supermarkets or a Mexican grocery store.

Cornmeal Pizza Dough
  (see recipe, page 4)
1 **pound bulk chorizo, Italian sausage,**
  or pork sausage
½ **cup chopped onion**
1 **16-ounce jar salsa or picante sauce**
2 **tablespoons snipped fresh cilantro**
  (optional)
1 **15-ounce can pinto beans, rinsed and**
  drained
2 **4-ounce cans whole green chili**
  peppers, cut into strips
2 **cups shredded Cojack cheese**
  (8 ounces)

Prepare Cornmeal Pizza Dough. Grease two 11- to 13-inch pizza pans or baking sheets. On a lightly floured surface, roll each half of dough into a circle 1 inch larger than pizza pan. Transfer dough to pans. Build up edges slightly. Prick generously with a fork. Do not let rise. Bake in a 425° oven for 10 to 12 minutes or till lightly browned.

Meanwhile, in a large skillet cook chorizo or sausage and onion till meat is brown and onion is tender. Drain fat. Pat with paper towels to remove additional fat.

Spread salsa or picante sauce over hot crusts. Sprinkle with cilantro, if desired. Top with chorizo mixture and pinto beans. Arrange green chili pepper strips atop the chorizo mixture and beans. Sprinkle with cheese. Bake about 12 minutes more or till cheese melts and sauce is bubbly. Makes 6 servings.

Nutrition information per serving: 509 calories, 35 g protein, 67 g carbohydrate, 42 g fat (16 g saturated), 35 mg cholesterol, 1,236 mg sodium, 702 mg potassium.

TWO PIZZAS IN ONE

Two pizzas are better than one—especially when they're served sandwich-style, like these frozen pizzas.

½ pound bulk Italian sausage or ground beef
2 15- to 15½-ounce frozen cheese pizzas
½ cup chopped green pepper
1 2-ounce can mushroom stems and pieces, drained
1 cup shredded Cojack cheese (4 ounces)

Cook Italian sausage or ground beef till brown. Drain fat.

Place *one* cheese pizza on a greased baking sheet. Top with cooked sausage or beef, green pepper, and mushrooms. Top with remaining cheese pizza, crust side up. Cover pizza with foil.

Bake in a 375° oven for 30 minutes. Remove foil and bake for 10 minutes more. Sprinkle shredded cheese over pizza. Bake about 5 minutes more or till cheese melts. Makes 6 servings.

Nutrition information per serving: 485 calories, 28 g protein, 49 g carbohydrate, 20 g fat (10 g saturated), 59 mg cholesterol, 1,160 mg sodium, 398 mg potassium.

PIZZA PIE

Use a fluted pastry wheel to make decorative cuts in the top crust.

1   15-ounce package (2 crusts) folded
    refrigerated unbaked piecrusts
1   tablespoon cornmeal
½   pound bulk Italian sausage or pork
    sausage
½   of a 3½-ounce package sliced
    pepperoni
1   4-ounce can mushroom stems and
    pieces, drained
2   cups shredded mozzarella and/or
    cheddar cheese (8 ounces)
1   cup Hot and Spicy Pizza Sauce
    (see recipe, page 5)
1   teaspoon milk or water

Let piecrusts stand at room temperature according to package directions. Lightly grease a 9-inch pie plate. Sprinkle pie plate with cornmeal. Set aside.

Meanwhile, cook sausage till brown; add pepperoni and heat through. Drain fat. Pat dry with paper towels to remove additional fat. Stir in mushrooms.

Unfold pie crusts. Transfer *one* of the crusts to prepared pie plate. Sprinkle *one-third* of the shredded cheese over bottom crust. Pour *half* of the Hot and Spicy Pizza Sauce over cheese. Top with the sausage-pepperoni mixture, another *one-third* of the shredded cheese, and the remaining Hot and Spicy Pizza Sauce. Top with remaining shredded cheese.

Cut several slits in remaining crust. Place top crust on filling. Trim and flute edge. Brush with milk or water.

Bake in a 425° oven about 30 minutes or till pastry is golden and pie is heated through. Let stand 10 minutes before serving. Cut into wedges. Makes 6 servings.

Nutrition information per serving: 588 calories, 20 g protein, 41 g carbohydrate, 38 g fat (8 g saturated), 70 mg cholesterol, 1,177 mg sodium, 392 mg potassium.

HAM AND POTATO BRUNCH PIZZA

A breakfast-style ham and potato combo and a sour cream sauce cover these pizza squares.

1　16-ounce loaf frozen bread dough,
　　thawed
2　medium potatoes, finely chopped
　　(2 cups)
1　medium red or green sweet pepper,
　　cut into bite-size strips
½　cup sliced green onion
2　tablespoons margarine or butter
½　cup mayonnaise or salad dressing
½　cup dairy sour cream
2　tablespoons snipped fresh parsley
¼　teaspoon pepper
1½　cups diced fully cooked ham
1　cup shredded cheddar or Swiss cheese
　　(4 ounces)

On a lightly floured surface, roll bread dough into a 16 x 12-inch rectangle. Press dough into the bottom and up the sides of a greased 15x10x1-inch baking pan. Prick generously with a fork. Bake in a 375° oven about 20 minutes or till light brown.

Meanwhile, in a large nonstick or well-seasoned skillet cook potatoes, sweet pepper, and green onion in margarine or butter over medium heat for 8 to 10 minutes or till tender, stirring often.

In a medium mixing bowl stir together mayonnaise or salad dressing, sour cream, parsley, and pepper; spread over hot crust. Top with potato mixture and ham. Sprinkle with cheddar or Swiss cheese.

Bake about 12 minutes more or till cheese melts and pizza is heated through. Makes 6 servings.

Nutrition information per serving: 553 calories, 22 g protein, 44 g carbohydrate, 32 g fat (10 g saturated), 59 mg cholesterol, 808 mg sodium, 439 mg potassium.

HAWAIIAN PINEAPPLE PIZZA

To give your pizza crust a different look (as shown in the photograph) snip the edges of the dough with scissors before baking.

1   16-ounce package hot roll mix
1   cup Herbed Pizza Sauce
     (see recipe, page 5) or one 8-ounce
     can pizza sauce
½   pound thinly sliced fully cooked ham,
     cut into ½ inch strips
1   green pepper, sliced into thin rings
1   20-ounce can pineapple tidbits,
     drained
1   cup shredded mozzarella cheese
     (4 ounces)
2   tablespoons grated Parmesan or
     Romano cheese

Grease a 13-inch pizza pan; set aside. Prepare hot roll mix according to package directions for pizza crust. Shape dough into a ball. On a lightly floured surface, roll dough into a circle 1 inch larger than pizza pan. Transfer dough to pizza pan. Build up edges slightly. Prick generously with a fork. Do not let rise. Bake in a 425° oven for 10 to 12 minutes or till lightly browned.

Spread pizza sauce over hot crust. Top with ham, green pepper rings, and pineapple tidbits. Sprinkle with mozzarella cheese and Parmesan or Romano cheese. Bake about 12 minutes more or till cheese melts and sauce is bubbly. Makes 4 to 5 servings.

Nutrition information per serving: 758 calories, 40 g protein, 112 g carbohydrate, 18 g fat (6 g saturated), 50 mg cholesterol, 1,910 mg sodium, 613 mg potassium.

CHEF'S SALAD PIZZA SQUARES

Is it a salad or is it a pizza? You decide.

½ of a 17½-ounce package (1 sheet) frozen puff pastry
2 cups torn mixed greens
4 ounces fully cooked ham, chicken, or beef, cut into thin strips
1 medium yellow or red sweet pepper, cut into bite-size strips
1 cup cherry tomatoes, cut into wedges
½ cup soft-style cream cheese with chives and onion
2 tablespoons milk
2 teaspoons coarse-grain brown mustard
1 tablespoon milk
1½ cups shredded Gruyère cheese (6 ounces)
1 or 2 hard-cooked eggs, cut into wedges (optional)

Thaw pastry according to package directions; cut pastry into 4 squares. Place pastry squares on a large baking sheet. Use a fork to generously prick pastry squares. Bake in a 375° oven for 20 to 25 minutes or till golden brown (pastry will shrink). Cool.

Meanwhile, in a large mixing bowl combine greens; ham, chicken, or beef; sweet pepper strips; and cherry tomato wedges.

For dressing, in a small mixing bowl stir together cream cheese, the 2 tablespoons milk, and mustard. Spoon *half* of the dressing over the greens mixture, tossing to coat. Stir the 1 tablespoon milk into the remaining dressing; set aside.

Preheat broiler. Sprinkle *1 cup* of the Gruyère cheese over the baked pastry squares. Broil 4 inches from heat about 1 minute or till cheese melts. Divide greens mixture evenly among pastry squares. Sprinkle with remaining Gruyère cheese. Broil for 1 to 2 minutes more or till cheese melts. Serve with remaining dressing. If desired, garnish with hard-cooked eggs. Makes 4 servings.

Nutrition information per serving: 619 calories, 26 g protein, 30 g carbohydrate, 44 g fat (14 g saturated), 93 mg cholesterol, 906 mg sodium, 480 mg potassium.

CANADIAN BACON AND SAUERKRAUT PIZZA

Serve this German-influenced pizza with ice-cold beer.

1 16-ounce loaf frozen whole wheat bread dough, thawed
1 8-ounce can pizza sauce
1 cup sauerkraut, rinsed, snipped, and well drained
8 ounces Canadian-style bacon, cut into thin slices
1 small onion, thinly sliced and separated into rings
1 cup shredded Monterey Jack or mozzarella cheese (4 ounces)
½ teaspoon caraway seed
    Fresh oregano sprig (optional)

On a lightly floured surface, roll bread dough into a 14-inch circle. Transfer to a greased 13-inch pizza pan. Build up edges slightly. Prick generously with a fork. Bake in a 375° oven for 20 to 25 minutes or till light brown.

Spread pizza sauce over hot crust. Top with sauerkraut, Canadian-style bacon, and onion rings. Sprinkle with Monterey Jack or mozzarella cheese and caraway seed. Bake about 10 minutes more or till cheese melts and sauce is bubbly. If desired, garnish with fresh oregano. Makes 6 servings.

Nutrition information per serving: 382 calories, 23 g protein, 49 g carbohydrate, 10 g fat (5 g saturated), 39 mg cholesterol, 1,426 mg sodium, 216 mg potassium.

EASY PITA PIZZAS

For a speedy weeknight supper, serve these pizzas along with some crunchy carrot and celery sticks.

4   large pita bread rounds
½   pound ground raw turkey or chicken
¾   cup sliced fresh mushrooms
⅔   cup chopped green pepper
⅔   cup chopped onion
2   cloves garlic, minced
1   cup Herbed Pizza Sauce
      (see recipe, page 5) or one 8-ounce
      can pizza sauce
½   teaspoon dried oregano, crushed
1   cup shredded mozzarella cheese
      (4 ounces)

Place pita bread rounds on a baking sheet. Broil 3 to 4 inches from heat about 1 minute on each side or till toasted. Set aside.

In a large skillet cook ground turkey or chicken, mushrooms, green pepper, onion, and garlic till turkey is brown and vegetables are tender. Drain fat, if necessary. Stir in pizza sauce and oregano. Cook and stir till bubbly.

Divide turkey mixture evenly between the toasted pita bread rounds. Sprinkle with mozzarella cheese. Return to broiler. Broil 3 to 4 inches from heat for 1 to 2 minutes or till cheese melts. Makes 4 servings.

Nutrition information per serving: 318 calories, 21 g protein, 34 g carbohydrate, 11 g fat (4 g saturated), 37 mg cholesterol, 631 mg sodium, 573 mg potassium.

SWEET PEPPER, CORN, AND TURKEY PIZZA

This trendy pizza requires a double recipe of the creamy Parmesan Pizza Sauce.

Cornmeal Pizza Dough
    (see recipe, page 4)
1 large sweet onion, sliced
1 large red and/or green sweet pepper,
    thinly sliced into rings
1 clove garlic, minced
1 tablespoon olive oil or cooking oil
1 10-ounce package frozen whole kernel
    corn, thawed
1 tablespoon snipped fresh basil or
    1 teaspoon dried basil, crushed
1 tablespoon snipped fresh oregano or
    1 teaspoon dried oregano, crushed
¼ teaspoon salt
¼ teaspoon crushed red pepper
2 cups Parmesan Pizza Sauce
    (see recipe, page 5)
2 cups cooked turkey or chicken cut
    into bite-size strips
2 cups shredded Monterey Jack or
    Muenster cheese (8 ounces)

Prepare Cornmeal Pizza Dough. Grease two 11- to 13-inch pizza pans or baking sheets. On a lightly floured surface, roll each half of dough into a circle 1 inch larger than pizza pan. Transfer to pans. Build up edges slightly. Flute and score edges, if desired. Prick generously with a fork. Do not let rise. Bake in a 425° oven for 10 to 12 minutes or till lightly browned.

Meanwhile, in a large skillet cook onion, sweet pepper, and garlic in hot oil till tender. Remove from heat; stir in corn, basil, oregano, salt, and crushed red pepper.

Spread Parmesan Pizza Sauce over hot crusts. Spoon corn mixture over sauce. Top with turkey or chicken. Sprinkle with cheese. Bake about 12 minutes more or till cheese melts and sauce is bubbly. Makes 6 servings.

Nutrition information per serving: 606 calories, 30 g protein, 63 g carbohydrate, 26 g fat (11 g saturated), 81 mg cholesterol, 971 mg sodium, 572 mg potassium.

CHICKEN-ARTICHOKE PIZZA

The 12-inch Italian bread shell, also known as Boboli, makes an easy crust for this pizza that's generously topped with chicken and vegetables.

1   6½-ounce jar marinated artichoke hearts
¾   pound boneless skinless chicken breast halves
2   medium zucchini and/or yellow summer squash, thinly sliced
1   small red or green sweet pepper, chopped
1   tablespoon olive oil or cooking oil
1½   cups sliced fresh mushrooms
2   green onions, thinly sliced
2   plum or small common tomatoes, sliced
1   2¼-ounce can sliced pitted ripe olives
3   tablespoons vinegar
½   teaspoon garlic powder
½   teaspoon seasoned salt
½   teaspoon dried oregano, crushed
½   teaspoon dried basil, crushed
1   tablespoon cornstarch
1   tablespoon water
1   16-ounce package Boboli (12-inch Italian bread shell)
1½   cups shredded mozzarella cheese (6 ounces)
¼   cup grated Parmesan cheese

Drain artichoke hearts, reserving liquid. Cut artichoke hearts into bite-size pieces; set aside.

Rinse chicken; pat dry. Cut into cubes and set aside.

In a large skillet cook and stir zucchini and sweet pepper in hot oil till crisp-tender; remove from skillet. Add mushrooms and green onions to skillet. Cook and stir till just tender; remove from skillet.

In the same skillet cook chicken, half at a time, for 2 to 3 minutes or till no longer pink. Return all chicken to skillet. Stir in reserved artichoke hearts and liquid, tomatoes, olives, vinegar, garlic powder, seasoned salt, oregano, and basil. Combine cornstarch and water; add to skillet. Cook and stir till thickened and bubbly. Cook and stir 1 minute more. Return all vegetables to skillet; stir till combined.

Place bread shell on a lightly greased baking sheet. Top with chicken mixture. Sprinkle with mozzarella cheese and Parmesan cheese.

Bake in a 425° oven for 10 to 12 minutes or till mozzarella cheese melts and pizza is heated through. Let stand 5 minutes before serving. Makes 6 servings.

Nutrition information per serving: 491 calories, 34 g protein, 42 g carbohydrate, 23 g fat (7 g saturated), 71 mg cholesterol, 937 mg sodium, 459 mg potassium.

CALIFORNIA-STYLE CHICKEN PIZZA

This newfangled pizza is topped with grilled chicken breasts, but you could use deli-roasted chicken if you're short on time.

1   16-ounce loaf frozen bread dough, thawed
¼   teaspoon finely shredded lemon peel
1   tablespoon lemon juice
1   tablespoon margarine or butter, melted
¾   pound boneless skinless chicken breast halves
¼   cup finely snipped dried tomatoes
    Parmesan Pizza Sauce
      (see recipe, page 5)
2   fresh medium tomatoes, thinly sliced
1   cup shredded Monterey Jack cheese (4 ounces)
½   cup alfalfa sprouts

On a lightly floured surface, roll bread dough into a 14-inch circle. Transfer dough to a greased 13-inch pizza pan. Build up edges slightly. Prick generously with a fork. Bake in a 375° oven for 20 to 25 minutes or till light brown.

In a small mixing bowl stir together lemon peel, lemon juice, and margarine or butter.

Rinse chicken breast halves; pat dry. Grill chicken directly over medium coals for 12 to 15 minutes or till chicken is tender and no longer pink, turning once halfway through grilling and brushing occasionally with lemon mixture the last 10 minutes of grilling. Cut chicken into cubes.

Meanwhile, pour enough boiling water over dried tomatoes to cover; let stand for 2 minutes. Drain well.

Spread Parmesan Pizza Sauce over hot crust. Top with chicken cubes, sliced fresh tomatoes, and dried tomatoes. Sprinkle with Monterey Jack cheese.

Bake about 12 minutes more or till cheese melts and sauce is bubbly. Top with alfalfa sprouts. Makes 6 servings.

Nutrition information per serving: 409 calories, 25 g protein, 40 g carbohydrate, 13 g fat (6 g saturated), 53 mg cholesterol, 358 mg sodium, 366 mg potassium.

SOUTHWESTERN GARDEN PIZZA

Bean dip and picante sauce help this yummy pizza live up to its geographical name, while the zucchini and green onion take care of the "garden" part.

Cornmeal Pizza Dough
(see recipe, page 4)
1 pound boneless skinless chicken
breast halves
1 tablespoon cooking oil
1 medium zucchini or yellow summer
squash, cut into 2-inch long
julienne strips (about 1½ cups)
2 green onions, bias sliced into 1-inch
pieces (½ cup)
1 9-ounce can bean dip
¾ cup picante sauce or salsa
2 cups shredded Monterey Jack cheese
(8 ounces)
2 green onions, thinly sliced

Prepare Cornmeal Pizza Dough. Grease two 11- to 13-inch pizza pans or baking sheets. On a lightly floured surface, roll each half of dough into a circle 1 inch larger than pizza pan. Transfer dough to pans. Build up edges slightly. Flute edges, if desired. Prick generously with a fork. Do not let rise. Bake in a 425° oven for 10 to 12 minutes or till lightly browned.

Meanwhile, rinse chicken; pat dry. Cut chicken into bite-size strips; set aside. Heat cooking oil in a 12-inch skillet over medium-high heat. Cook and stir zucchini or yellow summer squash in hot oil for 30 seconds. Add the 1-inch bias-sliced green onion pieces; cook and stir for 1 to 2 minutes or till all the vegetables are crisp-tender. Remove vegetables from the skillet. Add *half* of the chicken to the hot skillet. Stir-fry for 2 to 3 minutes or till no longer pink. Remove chicken from skillet. Repeat with the remaining chicken.

Spread bean dip over hot crusts. Spread picante sauce or salsa over bean dip. Spoon chicken and vegetables over picante sauce. Sprinkle with Monterey Jack cheese. Bake about 12 minutes more or till cheese melts and sauce is bubbly. Sprinkle with sliced green onion. Makes 6 to 8 servings.

Nutrition information per serving: 552 calories, 32 g protein, 51 g carbohydrate, 23 g fat (9 g saturated), 75 mg cholesterol, 793 mg sodium, 516 mg potassium.

CHEESY CHICKEN-VEGETABLE PIZZA

Mozzarella is the cheese of choice for most pizzas, but other cheeses, such as Muenster, Monterey Jack, and cheddar, also can be used because of their good melting qualities.

Garlic and Herb Pizza Dough
   (see recipe, page 4)
1 pound boneless skinless chicken
   breast halves
2 teaspoons lemon-pepper seasoning
2 tablespoons olive oil or cooking oil
   Herbed Pizza Sauce (see recipe,
   page 5) or one 15-ounce can or
   one 15½-ounce jar pizza sauce
2 small green peppers, cut into bite-size
   strips
1 medium red onion, sliced and
   separated into rings
1 cup sliced fresh mushrooms
1 2¼-ounce can sliced pitted ripe olives,
   drained
¼ cup grated Parmesan or Romano
   cheese
2 tablespoons snipped fresh basil or
   2 teaspoons dried basil, crushed
1 cup shredded Muenster cheese
   (4 ounces)
1 cup shredded Monterey Jack cheese
   (4 ounces)

Prepare Garlic and Herb Pizza Dough. Grease two 11- to 13-inch pizza pans or baking sheets. On a lightly floured surface, roll each half of dough into a circle 1 inch larger than pizza pan. Transfer dough to pans. Build up edges slightly; flute edges, if desired. Prick generously with a fork. Do not let rise. Bake in a 425° oven for 10 to 12 minutes or till lightly browned.

Meanwhile, rinse chicken; pat dry. Sprinkle both sides of chicken breast halves with lemon-pepper seasoning, pressing seasoning into the surface of the chicken. In a large skillet cook chicken in hot oil over medium heat for 8 to 10 minutes or till chicken is tender and no longer pink, turning often to brown evenly. Remove from skillet. Cut chicken into bite-size pieces.

Spread pizza sauce over hot crusts. Top with chicken pieces, green pepper strips, onion rings, mushrooms, and olives. Sprinkle with Parmesan or Romano cheese and basil. Sprinkle with Muenster cheese and Monterey Jack cheese. Bake about 12 minutes more or till cheese melts and sauce is bubbly. Makes 6 servings.

Nutrition information per serving: 612 calories, 34 g protein, 55 g carbohydrate, 29 g fat (11 g saturated), 78 mg cholesterol, 1,196 mg sodium, 708 mg potassium.

SEAFOOD-ARTICHOKE PIZZA

This easy seafood pizza features crab-flavored fish pieces that are sometimes called surimi. This "seafood" is actually processed fish that's been flavored and shaped to make imitation seafood products.

1 10-ounce package refrigerated pizza dough
1 9-ounce package frozen artichoke hearts
1 14½-ounce can pizza-style chunky tomatoes
1 8-ounce package frozen, crab-flavored, fish pieces, thawed and cut into 2-inch pieces, or one 6-ounce package frozen cooked shrimp, thawed
½ cup grated Parmesan cheese

Lightly grease an 11- to 13-inch pizza pan. Unroll pizza dough and transfer to greased pan, pressing dough out with your hands. Build up edges slightly. Prick generously with a fork. Bake in a 425° oven for 7 to 10 minutes or till lightly browned.

Meanwhile, cook artichoke hearts according to package directions. Cut any large artichoke hearts into bite-size pieces.

Spread pizza-style chunky tomatoes over hot crust. Arrange artichoke hearts and fish pieces or shrimp atop tomatoes. Sprinkle with Parmesan cheese. Bake for 5 to 7 minutes more or till heated through. Makes 4 servings.

Nutrition information per serving: 444 calories, 21 g protein, 68 g carbohydrate, 10 g fat (3 g saturated), 18 mg cholesterol, 1,502 mg sodium, 660 mg potassium.

SHRIMP AND FETA CHEESE PIZZA WITH ROSEMARY

For your next party, cut this contemporary pizza into 16 wedges and serve it as an appetizer.

8　ounces fresh or frozen peeled and
　　deveined shrimp
　　Garlic and Herb Pizza Dough
　　(see recipe, page 4)
2　cloves garlic, minced
1　tablespoon olive oil or cooking oil
1½　cups shredded mozzarella cheese
　　(6 ounces)
1　2¼-ounce can sliced pitted ripe olives,
　　drained
½　cup crumbled feta cheese
¼　cup sliced green onion
1　tablespoon snipped fresh rosemary or
　　1 teaspoon dried rosemary, crushed

Thaw shrimp, if frozen. Halve shrimp lengthwise; set aside.

Prepare Garlic and Herb Pizza Dough. Grease two 11- to 13-inch pizza pans or baking sheets. On a lightly floured surface, roll each half of dough into a circle 1 inch larger than pizza pan. Transfer dough to pans. Build up edges slightly. Flute edges, if desired. Prick generously with a fork. Do not let rise. Bake in a 425° oven for 10 to 12 minutes or till lightly browned.

Meanwhile, in a large skillet cook shrimp and garlic in olive oil for 1 to 2 minutes or till shrimp turn pink, stirring frequently.

Sprinkle mozzarella cheese over hot crusts. Spoon shrimp mixture over mozzarella cheese. Sprinkle with olives, feta cheese, green onion, and rosemary.

Bake for 10 to 12 minutes more or till mozzarella cheese melts and pizza is heated through. Makes 6 servings.

Nutrition information per serving: 403 calories, 21 g protein, 43 g carbohydrate, 17 g fat (6 g saturated), 82 mg cholesterol, 463 mg sodium, 185 mg potassium.

TUNA AND ROASTED SWEET PEPPER PIZZA

For an elegant touch, sprinkle 1 tablespoon of capers atop this updated pizza.

1 **10-ounce package refrigerated pizza dough**
   Parmesan Pizza Sauce (see recipe, page 5) or 1 cup refrigerated Alfredo pasta sauce
1 **6½-ounce can chunk white tuna, drained and broken into chunks**
1 **7-ounce jar roasted red sweet peppers, drained and cut into bite-size strips**
1 **cup shredded mozzarella cheese (4 ounces)**

Lightly grease an 11- to 13-inch pizza pan. Unroll pizza dough and transfer to greased pan, pressing dough out with your hands. Build up edges slightly. Prick generously with a fork. Bake in a 425° oven for 7 to 10 minutes or till lightly browned.

Spread Parmesan Pizza Sauce or refrigerated Alfredo pasta sauce over the hot crust. Top with tuna and roasted red pepper strips. Sprinkle with mozzarella cheese.

Bake for 10 to 12 minutes more or till cheese melts and sauce is bubbly. Makes 4 servings.

Nutrition information per serving: 391 calories, 28 g protein, 36 g carbohydrate, 15 g fat (6 g saturated), 44 mg cholesterol, 775 mg sodium, 414 mg potassium.

PIZZA WITH FOUR CHEESES AND PLUM TOMATOES

Plum tomatoes are meaty, oval-shaped tomatoes with little juice and a mild, rich flavor. They also are called Italian or Roma tomatoes.

1 16-ounce loaf frozen bread dough, thawed
2 large green and/or red sweet peppers, chopped (2 cups)
1 cup shredded mozzarella cheese (4 ounces)
¾ cup shredded fontina cheese (3 ounces)
½ cup grated Parmesan cheese (2 ounces)
½ cup crumbled feta cheese (2 ounces)
2 tablespoons snipped fresh parsley
1 tablespoon snipped fresh basil or 1 teaspoon dried basil, crushed
3 medium plum tomatoes or small common tomatoes, thinly sliced
1 tablespoon olive oil or cooking oil
2 cloves garlic, minced

On a lightly floured surface, roll bread dough into a 14-inch circle. Transfer dough to a greased 13-inch pizza pan. Build up edges slightly. Prick generously with a fork. Bake in a 375° oven for 20 to 25 minutes or till light brown.

Sprinkle chopped sweet peppers over hot crust. Top with mozzarella cheese, fontina cheese, Parmesan cheese, and feta cheese. Sprinkle parsley and basil over cheeses. Arrange tomato slices on top. In a small mixing bowl combine olive oil and garlic. Brush tomato slices with oil mixture.

Bake 15 to 20 minutes more or till cheeses melt and pizza is heated through. Let stand 5 minutes before serving. Makes 6 servings.

Nutrition information per serving: 379 calories, 19 g protein, 37 g carbohydrate, 17 g fat (6 g saturated), 42 mg cholesterol, 382 mg sodium, 215 mg potassium.

GRILLED SHRIMP AND PEPPERONI PIZZA

Cooking this pizza over the coals makes for an extra-crispy crust.

1 cup broccoli flowerets
1 small zucchini, quartered lengthwise and sliced
1 10-ounce package refrigerated pizza dough
¾ cup pizza sauce or ⅓ cup purchased pesto
¾ pound peeled, cooked shrimp
½ of a 3½-ounce package sliced pepperoni
1½ cups shredded mozzarella cheese (6 ounces)

Cook broccoli and zucchini in enough boiling water to cover for 2 minutes. Drain and rinse immediately in cold water. Set aside.

Lightly grease an 11- to 13-inch pizza pan. Unroll pizza dough and transfer to greased pan, pressing out dough with your hands. Build up edges slightly. Prick generously with a fork.

Place pizza pan on the grill rack directly over medium coals. Cover grill and grill for 5 minutes. Carefully remove pan from grill.

Spread pizza sauce or pesto over hot crust. Top with cooked vegetables, shrimp, and pepperoni. Sprinkle with mozzarella cheese. Return pizza to grill rack. Grill, covered, about 10 minutes more or till cheese melts and pizza is heated through, checking occasionally to make sure crust doesn't overbrown. Makes 6 servings.

Nutrition information per serving: 289 calories, 24 g protein, 23 g carbohydrate, 11 g fat (4 g saturated), 127 mg cholesterol, 726 mg sodium, 440 mg potassium.

MEXICAN BLACK BEAN PIZZA

The beans and cheese provide more than enough protein in this meatless pizza.

1 10-ounce package refrigerated pizza dough
1 15-ounce can black beans, rinsed and drained
2 tablespoons snipped fresh cilantro or parsley
2 tablespoons salsa
1 teaspoon ground cumin
¼ teaspoon bottled hot pepper sauce
2 cloves garlic, quartered
1½ cups shredded Cojack or cheddar cheese (6 ounces)
½ cup chopped red sweet pepper
¼ cup sliced green onion
½ cup dairy sour cream
2 tablespoons salsa

Lightly grease an 11- to 13-inch pizza pan. Unroll pizza dough and transfer to greased pan, pressing dough out with your hands. Build up edges slightly. Prick generously with a fork. Bake in a 425° oven for 7 to 10 minutes or till lightly browned.

Meanwhile, in a blender container or food processor bowl combine black beans, cilantro or parsley, 2 tablespoons salsa, cumin, hot pepper sauce, and garlic. Cover and blend or process till smooth, stopping to scrape down sides if necessary.

Spread bean mixture over hot crust. Sprinkle with Cojack or cheddar cheese, chopped red sweet pepper, and green onion. Bake about 10 minutes more or till cheese melts and pizza is heated through.

In a small bowl combine sour cream and 2 tablespoons salsa. Serve pizza with sour cream mixture. Makes 4 servings.

Nutrition information per serving: 468 calories, 24 g protein, 51 g carbohydrate, 20 g fat (11 g saturated), 50 mg cholesterol, 917 mg sodium, 430 mg potassium.

VEGETARIAN PIZZA

When summer rolls around and zucchini, yellow summer squash, and tomatoes are at their peak, enjoy this garden-fresh pizza often.

1   16-ounce loaf frozen whole wheat
    bread dough, thawed
1   small zucchini, chopped (about 1 cup)
1   small yellow summer squash, chopped
    (about 1 cup)
¼   teaspoon crushed red pepper
2   cloves garlic, minced
1   tablespoon olive oil or cooking oil
2   cups shredded mozzarella cheese
    (8 ounces)
2   medium red and/or yellow tomatoes,
    thinly sliced
2   tablespoons grated Parmesan or
    Romano cheese

On a lightly floured surface, roll bread dough into a 14-inch circle. Transfer to a greased 13-inch pizza pan. Build up edges slightly. Prick dough generously with a fork. Bake in a 375° oven for 20 to 25 minutes or till light brown.

Meanwhile, in a large skillet cook zucchini, summer squash, crushed red pepper, and garlic in hot oil about 5 minutes or till vegetables are almost tender. Drain.

Sprinkle *1 cup* of the mozzarella cheese over hot crust. Arrange tomato slices in a circular pattern atop cheese. Top with zucchini mixture. Sprinkle with remaining mozzarella cheese and Parmesan or Romano cheese. Bake about 12 minutes more or till cheese melts and pizza is heated through. Makes 6 servings.

Nutrition information per serving: 320 calories, 16 g protein, 37 g carbohydrate, 9 g fat (5 g saturated), 23 mg cholesterol, 220 mg sodium, 198 mg potassium.

PIZZA À LA CARBONARA

You'll find this pizza every bit as rich and cheesy as the Italian pasta specialty it's named after.

1   10-ounce package refrigerated pizza
       dough
     Parmesan Pizza Sauce
       (see recipe, page 5)
½   pound (10 to 11 slices) bacon, crisp-
       cooked, drained, and crumbled
1   cup sliced fresh mushrooms
3   green onions, sliced
1½ cups shredded Monterey Jack cheese
       (6 ounces)

Lightly grease an 11- to 13-inch pizza pan. Unroll pizza dough and transfer to greased pan, pressing dough out with your hands. Build up edges slightly. Prick generously with a fork. Bake in a 425° oven for 7 to 10 minutes or till lightly browned.

Spread Parmesan Pizza Sauce over hot crust. Top with bacon, mushrooms, and green onions. Sprinkle with Monterey Jack cheese. Bake about 12 minutes more or till cheese melts and sauce is bubbly. Let stand 5 minutes before serving. Makes 4 servings.

Nutrition information per serving: 502 calories, 25 g protein, 34 g carbohydrate, 30 g fat (14 g saturated), 61 mg cholesterol, 942 mg sodium, 375 mg potassium.

POPOVER PIZZA CASSEROLE

For this homestyle dish, a saucy turkey and pepperoni mixture is topped with a layer of mozzarella cheese and a popover batter that puffs while it bakes.

1   pound ground raw turkey or
      ground beef
1   cup chopped onion
1   cup chopped green pepper
½   of a 3½-ounce package sliced
      pepperoni, halved
1   15-ounce can or one 15½-ounce jar
      pizza sauce
1   2-ounce can mushroom stems and
      pieces, drained
½   teaspoon fennel seed, crushed
½   teaspoon dried oregano, crushed
½   teaspoon dried basil, crushed
2   eggs
1   cup milk
1   tablespoon cooking oil
1   cup all-purpose flour
1   6-ounce package thinly sliced
      mozzarella cheese
¼   cup grated Parmesan cheese

In a large skillet cook turkey or beef, onion, and green pepper till meat is brown and vegetables are tender. Drain fat. Cut pepperoni slices in half. Stir pepperoni, pizza sauce, mushrooms, fennel seed, oregano, and basil into meat mixture. Bring to boiling. Reduce heat and simmer, uncovered, for 10 minutes, stirring occasionally.

Meanwhile, for topping, in a small bowl combine eggs, milk, and oil. Beat with an electric mixer on medium speed for 1 minute. Add flour; beat 1 minute more or till smooth.

Grease the sides of a 13x9x2-inch baking dish; spoon meat mixture into dish. Arrange cheese slices over hot meat mixture. Pour topping over cheese, covering completely. Sprinkle with Parmesan cheese.

Bake in a 400° oven for 25 to 30 minutes or till topping is puffed and golden brown. Serve immediately. Makes 8 servings.

Nutrition information per serving: 316 calories, 21 g protein, 22 g carbohydrate, 16 g fat (6 g saturated), 91 mg cholesterol, 688 mg sodium, 480 mg potassium.

STUFFED PIZZA BREAD

If you like, cut each crescent-shaped loaf into 12 slices and serve as an appetizer.

1 16-ounce package hot roll mix
1 pound bulk Italian sausage
1 cup finely chopped green or red sweet
  pepper
½ cup chopped onion
1 cup shredded mozzarella cheese
  (4 ounces)
1 teaspoon dried Italian seasoning,
  crushed
1 egg white
1 tablespoon water
2 teaspoons sesame seed

Prepare hot roll mix according to package directions for rolls through the kneading step. Cover; let rest.

Meanwhile, for filling, in a large skillet cook sausage, sweet pepper, and onion till sausage is brown and vegetables are tender. Drain fat. Pat with paper towels to remove additional fat. Add mozzarella cheese and Italian seasoning to sausage mixture; mix well.

Divide dough in half. On a lightly floured surface roll *one-half* of the dough into a 10x8-inch rectangle. Spoon *half* of the filling over the dough to within 1 inch of all edges. Beginning at one long edge, roll up the dough jelly-roll style. Moisten and pinch edges to seal. Repeat with the remaining dough and filling to make a second loaf.

Place each loaf, seam side down, on a greased baking sheet. Shape each loaf into a crescent. Using kitchen scissors, snip the top of each loaf in three places. Cover and let rise in a warm place about 20 minutes or till nearly doubled.

Just before baking, combine egg white and water. Brush the egg white mixture over the tops of the loaves. Sprinkle with sesame seed.

Bake in a 375° oven for 25 minutes or till bread is golden brown. Cut each loaf into 6 slices; serve warm. Makes 6 servings.

Nutrition information per serving: 567 calories, 28 g protein, 61 g carbohydrate, 23 g fat (7 g saturated), 87 mg cholesterol, 1,104 mg sodium, 401 mg potassium.

PIZZA QUICHE

Turn this quiche into a tasty breakfast dish by using Canadian-style bacon instead of pepperoni.

Pastry for Single-Crust Pie
1 cup shredded mozzarella cheese (4 ounces)
½ cup shredded cheddar cheese (2 ounces)
1 tablespoon all-purpose flour
3 beaten eggs
1½ cups milk
½ cup chopped pepperoni
1 2½-ounce jar sliced mushrooms, drained or ¼ cup sliced pitted ripe olives
½ teaspoon dried oregano, crushed
1 8-ounce can pizza sauce

Prepare Pastry for Single-Crust Pie. Ease pastry into a 10-inch tart pan with a removable bottom or a 10-inch quiche dish. Press pastry into fluted sides of tart pan or quiche dish and trim edges. Line the unpricked pastry shell with a double thickness of foil. Bake in a 450° oven for 8 minutes. Remove the foil. Bake for 4 to 5 minutes more or till pastry is set and dry. Remove pastry from oven. Reduce oven temperature to 325°.

In a medium mixing bowl toss together mozzarella cheese, cheddar cheese, and flour. Sprinkle cheese mixture over bottom of hot pastry shell. In a large mixing bowl stir together eggs, milk, pepperoni, mushrooms or olives, and oregano. Carefully pour egg mixture into pastry shell.

Bake in the 325° oven for 35 to 40 minutes or till a knife inserted near the center comes out clean. Let stand 10 minutes before serving. Meanwhile, heat the pizza sauce in small saucepan over medium heat. Serve quiche with pizza sauce. Makes 6 servings.

Pastry for Single-Crust Pie: In a large mixing bowl combine 1¼ cups *all-purpose flour* and ¼ teaspoon *salt*. Cut in ⅓ cup *shortening* till pieces are the size of small peas. Sprinkle 3 to 4 tablespoons *cold water,* 1 tablespoon at a time, over mixture, tossing with a fork after each addition till all is moistened. Form dough into a ball. On a lightly floured surface, flatten dough with hands. Roll dough from center to edges, forming a circle about 12 inches in diameter.

Nutrition information per serving: 427 calories, 18 g protein, 27 g carbohydrate, 27 g fat (10 g saturated), 141 mg cholesterol, 809 mg sodium, 380 mg potassium.

PIZZA BURGERS

If you can't make it outside to grill these burgers, broil them on the unheated rack of a broiler pan, 3 inches from the heat, for 14 to 18 minutes or till no pink remains, turning once halfway through broiling.

1   beaten egg
¼   cup fine dry bread crumbs
1   8-ounce can pizza sauce
½   teaspoon dried basil or oregano,
        crushed
¼   teaspoon salt
¼   teaspoon pepper
1   pound lean ground beef
2   ounces pepperoni, finely chopped
6   hamburger buns, split and toasted
⅓   cup shredded mozzarella cheese

In a medium mixing bowl combine egg, bread crumbs, *2 tablespoons* of the pizza sauce, basil or oregano, salt, and pepper. Add ground beef and pepperoni; mix well. Shape meat mixture into six ¾-inch-thick patties.

Grill burgers directly over medium coals for 14 to 18 minutes or till no pink remains, turning once halfway through grilling.

Meanwhile, in a small saucepan heat the remaining pizza sauce. Place burgers on the bottom halves of the buns. Spoon some of the remaining pizza sauce over the burgers. Sprinkle burgers with mozzarella cheese. Top with remaining bun halves. Pass any remaining pizza sauce. Makes 6 servings.

Nutrition information per serving: 373 calories, 23 g protein, 28 g carbohydrate, 18 g fat (7 g saturated), 93 mg cholesterol, 812 mg sodium, 419 mg potassium.

PIZZA STEW

This chunky sausage and vegetable stew will send the scents of pizza through your house as it simmers on your stove top.

¾ pound bulk pork sausage
1   cup sliced fresh mushrooms
½ cup chopped onion
2   cloves garlic, minced
1   28-ounce can whole tomatoes, cut up
2   cups loose-pack frozen broccoli, cauliflower, and carrots
1   15-ounce can or 15½-ounce jar pizza sauce
1½ cups tomato juice
1   teaspoon dried oregano, crushed
½ teaspoon fennel seed, crushed
6   slices French bread, toasted
1   cup shredded mozzarella cheese (4 ounces)

In a large saucepan cook sausage, mushrooms, onion, and garlic till meat is brown and onion is tender. Drain fat.

Stir in undrained tomatoes, frozen vegetables, pizza sauce, tomato juice, oregano, and fennel seed. Bring to boiling. Reduce heat. Cover and simmer for 15 minutes.

Meanwhile, sprinkle toasted bread with mozzarella cheese. Place bread under the broiler for 1 to 2 minutes or till cheese melts.

To serve, ladle the sausage mixture into bowls. Top each serving with a slice of toasted bread. Makes 6 servings.

Nutrition information per serving: 380 calories, 20 g protein, 40 g carbohydrate, 16 g fat (6 g saturated), 43 mg cholesterol, 1,529 mg sodium, 1,062 mg potassium.

CHEESY CALZONES

Calzones are pizzas that have been transformed into turnovers. The same dough and toppings that are used for pizzas can be used to make calzones.

Cheese Pizza Dough
(see recipe, page 4)
1 **cup shredded cheddar cheese**
(4 ounces)
1 **cup shredded Gruyère cheese**
(4 ounces)
1 **cup shredded fontina cheese**
(4 ounces)
½ **cup ricotta cheese**
½ **cup oil-packed dried tomatoes,**
drained and snipped
2 **teaspoons milk**
1 **cup Herbed Pizza Sauce**
(see recipe, page 5) or one 8-ounce
can pizza sauce

Prepare Cheese Pizza Dough. On a lightly floured surface, roll each half of dough into a 13-inch circle. Transfer dough to greased baking sheets. Set aside.

For filling, stir together cheddar cheese, Gruyère cheese, fontina cheese, ricotta cheese, and dried tomatoes. Spoon cheese mixture over *half* of *each* dough circle; spread to within 1 inch of edges.

Moisten edges of dough with water. Fold dough in half over filling. Seal edges by pressing with tines of a fork. Flute edges, if desired. Prick tops. Brush tops with milk.

Bake in a 375° oven for 30 to 35 minutes or till crust is lightly browned. Meanwhile, heat pizza sauce in a small saucepan over medium heat. Cut calzones into wedges. Serve calzones with pizza sauce. Makes 6 servings.

Nutrition information per serving: 579 calories, 28 g protein, 49 g carbohydrate, 30 g fat (15 g saturated), 76 mg cholesterol, 799 mg sodium, 478 mg potassium.

VEGETABLE-CHEESE CALZONES

Watch your tongue! Since fillings in calzones become very hot during baking, let calzones cool a little after you cut them open.

8   ounces ground beef or ground pork
½   cup chopped onion
1   14½-ounce can Italian-style stewed
      tomatoes
½   cup chopped broccoli
½   teaspoon dried Italian seasoning,
      crushed
¼   teaspoon pepper
¼   cup chopped green pepper
¼   cup sliced pitted ripe olives
2   10-ounce packages refrigerated pizza
      dough
1   cup shredded cheddar cheese
      (4 ounces)
2   teaspoons milk
¼   cup grated Parmesan cheese
      Pizza sauce (optional)

For filling, in a medium skillet cook beef or pork and onion till meat is brown and onion is tender. Drain fat. Stir in undrained tomatoes, broccoli, Italian seasoning, and pepper. Bring to boiling. Reduce heat. Simmer, uncovered, about 15 minutes or till most of the liquid has evaporated, stirring occasionally. Remove from heat. Stir in green pepper and olives.

Unroll *one* package pizza dough. On a lightly floured surface, roll dough into a 15x10-inch rectangle; cut into six 5-inch squares. Repeat with remaining package pizza dough.

Divide filling among the 12 squares; sprinkle with cheddar cheese. Brush edges with water. Lift one corner and stretch dough over to the opposite corner. Press edges of dough well with a fork to seal.

Arrange calzones on a greased baking sheet. Prick tops with a fork. Brush tops with milk; sprinkle with Parmesan cheese. Bake in a 425° oven about 10 minutes or till golden brown. Serve with pizza sauce, if desired. Makes 6 servings.

Nutrition information per serving: 449 calories, 23 g protein, 51 g carbohydrate, 16 g fat (7 g saturated), 47 mg cholesterol, 950 mg sodium, 459 mg potassium.

LAMB AND FETA CHEESE CALZONES

A pizza turnover with Greek overtones—lamb, black olives, and feta cheese.

Garlic and Herb Pizza Dough
   (see recipe, page 4)
1 **pound ground lamb or ground beef**
½ **cup chopped onion**
2 **cloves garlic, minced**
¼ **teaspoon ground cinnamon**
1 **cup Herbed Pizza Sauce**
   (see recipe, page 5) or one 8-ounce
   can pizza sauce
½ **cup sliced pitted ripe olives or sliced**
   fresh mushrooms
1 **cup crumbled feta cheese or shredded**
   provolone cheese (4 ounces)
2 **teaspoons milk**
1 **teaspoon sesame seed**

Prepare Garlic and Herb Pizza Dough. On a lightly floured surface, roll each half of dough into a 13-inch circle. Transfer to greased baking sheets. Set aside.

For filling, cook lamb or beef, onion, and garlic till meat is brown and onion is tender. Drain fat. Stir in cinnamon. Spread pizza sauce on *half* of *each* dough circle to within 1 inch of edge. Sprinkle meat mixture over sauce. Top with olives or mushrooms and feta or provolone cheese.

Moisten edges of dough with water. Fold dough in half over filling. Seal edges by pressing with tines of a fork. Flute edges, if desired. Cut slits in tops. Brush with milk; sprinkle with sesame seed.

Bake in a 375° oven for 30 to 35 minutes or till crust is lightly browned. Makes 6 servings.

Nutrition information per serving: 488 calories, 23 g protein, 48 g carbohydrate, 23 g fat (8 g saturated), 67 mg cholesterol, 567 mg sodium, 481 mg potassium.

DELI CALZONES

These tasty pockets of dough are stuffed with pepperoni, salami, spinach, and ricotta cheese.

Pizza Dough (see recipe, page 4)

1 10-ounce package frozen chopped spinach, thawed
1 cup ricotta cheese
1 3½-ounce package sliced pepperoni, chopped
3 ounces thinly sliced salami, chopped
⅓ cup grated Parmesan or Romano cheese
1 tablespoon snipped fresh basil or 1 teaspoon dried basil, crushed
¼ teaspoon garlic powder
¼ teaspoon pepper
2 teaspoons milk

Prepare Pizza Dough. On a lightly floured surface, roll each half of dough into a 13-inch circle. Transfer dough to greased baking sheets. Set aside.

For filling, pat spinach dry with paper towels. In a large mixing bowl stir together spinach, ricotta cheese, pepperoni, salami, Parmesan or Romano cheese, basil, garlic powder, and pepper. Spread filling on *half* of *each* dough circle to within 1-inch of edge.

Moisten edges of dough with water. Fold dough in half over filling. Seal edges by pressing with tines of a fork. Flute edges, if desired. Prick tops. Brush tops with milk.

Bake in a 375° oven for 30 to 35 minutes or till crust is lightly browned. Makes 6 servings.

Nutrition information per serving: 467 calories, 21 g protein, 46 g carbohydrate, 22 g fat (8 g saturated), 41 mg cholesterol, 932 mg sodium, 367 mg potassium.

ITALIAN SAUSAGE-MUSHROOM CALZONES

This flavorful calzone gets a double dose of zip from a spicy hot sauce and Italian sausage.

1 pound bulk Italian sausage
1 cup sliced fresh mushrooms
½ cup chopped onion
1 cup Hot and Spicy Pizza Sauce
      (see recipe, page 5) or one 8-ounce
      can pizza sauce
2 10-ounce packages refrigerated pizza
      dough
2 cups shredded mozzarella cheese
      (8 ounces)
2 teaspoons milk
2 tablespoons grated Parmesan or
      Romano cheese

In a large skillet cook sausage, mushrooms, and onion till sausage is brown and onion is tender. Drain fat. Pat with paper towels to remove additional fat. Stir in pizza sauce.

Unroll one package of pizza dough. On a lightly floured surface, roll dough into a 15x10-inch rectangle; cut into six 5-inch squares. Repeat with remaining package of pizza dough.

Divide meat mixture among the 12 squares; sprinkle with mozzarella cheese. Brush edges with water. Lift one corner and stretch dough over to the opposite corner. Seal edges by pressing with tines of fork.

Arrange calzones on a greased baking sheet. Prick tops with a fork. Brush tops with milk; sprinkle with Parmesan or Romano cheese. Bake in a 425° oven for 10 to 15 minutes or till golden brown. Makes 6 servings.

Nutrition information per serving: 566 calories, 30 g protein, 51 g carbohydrate, 25 g fat (9 g saturated), 66 mg cholesterol, 1,429 mg sodium, 503 mg potassium.

PIZZA MARGHERITA

This basil-scented pizza was invented and named for Italy's Queen Margherita who reigned in the 1800s.

Pizza Dough (see recipe, page 4)
1   **cup shredded mozzarella cheese**
     (4 ounces)
1   **ripe medium yellow tomato, thinly**
     sliced
1   **ripe medium red tomato, thinly sliced**
1   **tablespoon olive oil or cooking oil**
¼   **cup snipped fresh basil**
¼   **cup grated Parmesan cheese**

Prepare Pizza Dough. Grease an 11- to 13-inch pizza pan or baking sheet. On a lightly floured surface, roll *half* of the dough into a circle 1 inch larger than pizza pan. Transfer dough to pan. (Reserve remaining dough for another use.) Build up edges slightly. Prick generously with a fork. Do not let rise. Bake in a 425° oven for 10 to 12 minutes or till lightly browned.

Sprinkle mozzarella cheese over hot crust. Arrange tomato slices in a circular pattern atop cheese. Drizzle with oil. Sprinkle with fresh basil and Parmesan cheese.

Bake about 12 minutes more or till cheese melts and pizza is heated through. Makes 12 appetizer servings.

Nutrition information per serving: 167 calories, 6 g protein, 22 g carbohydrate, 6 g fat (2 g saturated), 7 mg cholesterol, 135 mg sodium, 100 mg potassium.

VEGETABLE PIZZA

Thanks to its no-measure ingredients, this appetizer pizza goes together fast.

1   10-ounce package refrigerated pizza
     dough
1   16-ounce package loose-pack frozen
     Italian-blend vegetables
1   8-ounce can pizza sauce
1   2½-ounce jar sliced mushrooms,
     drained
1   2¼-ounce can sliced pitted ripe olives,
     drained
1   8-ounce package shredded mozzarella
     cheese (2 cups)
     Grated Parmesan cheese (optional)
     Crushed red pepper (optional)

Lightly grease an 11- to 13-inch pizza pan. Unroll pizza dough and transfer to greased pan, pressing out dough with your hands. Build up edges slightly. Prick generously with a fork. Bake in a 425° oven for 7 to 10 minutes or till lightly browned.

Meanwhile, cook the frozen vegetables according to package directions till crisp-tender; drain well. Spread pizza sauce over hot crust. Top with cooked vegetables, mushrooms, and olives. Sprinkle with mozzarella cheese.

Bake for 10 to 12 minutes more or till cheese melts and sauce is bubbly. Sprinkle with Parmesan cheese and crushed red pepper, if desired. Makes 12 appetizer servings.

Nutrition information per serving: 139 calories, 8 g protein, 16 g carbohydrate, 5 g fat (2 g saturated), 11 mg cholesterol, 385 mg sodium, 187 mg potassium.

PIZZA QUESADILLAS

For a light lunch, serve these cheesy quesadillas with soup or a salad.

½ **cup pizza sauce**
6 **7-inch flour tortillas**
2 **cups shredded Monterey Jack cheese with jalapeño peppers or Monterey Jack cheese (8 ounces)**
⅓ **cup finely chopped pepperoni**
3 **tablespoons sliced pitted ripe olives**

Spread some of the pizza sauce on *half* of *each* tortilla. Sprinkle Monterey Jack cheese atop pizza sauce on each tortilla. Top with pepperoni and olives. Fold tortillas in half; press down edges gently.

In a large skillet or griddle cook tortillas, 2 or 3 at a time, over medium heat about 4 minutes or till cheese melts, turning once.

Cut each tortilla into three triangles. Makes 9 appetizer servings.

Nutrition information per serving: 194 calories, 9 g protein, 13 g carbohydrate, 12 g fat (6 g saturated), 27 mg cholesterol, 427 mg sodium, 109 mg potassium.

RATATOUILLE PIZZA

Besides every vowel in the alphabet, Italian ratatouille (raa taa TOO ee) also contains just about every vegetable from your garden. Although usually served as a side dish, ratatouille makes a delicious sauce for this colorful appetizer.

1 small eggplant (about ¾ pound)
½ cup chopped onion
2 cloves garlic, minced
2 tablespoons olive oil or cooking oil
4 medium red tomatoes, peeled, seeded, and chopped (about 2⅔ cups)
1 tablespoon snipped fresh oregano or thyme or 1 teaspoon dried oregano or thyme, crushed
½ teaspoon sugar
¼ teaspoon salt
⅛ teaspoon pepper
1 16-ounce package Boboli (12-inch Italian bread shell)
2 medium red and/or yellow tomatoes, halved lengthwise and thinly sliced
1 small zucchini, thinly sliced (2 cups)
1 small yellow summer squash, thinly sliced (2 cups)
½ cup crumbled feta cheese
2 tablespoons sliced pitted ripe olives
½ cup shredded mozzarella cheese (2 ounces)

Chop enough of the eggplant to make 1 cup. Halve remaining eggplant lengthwise and cut into thin slices; set aside.

In a medium skillet cook onion and garlic in 1 *tablespoon* of the oil till tender but not brown. Add chopped eggplant, chopped tomatoes, oregano or thyme, sugar, salt, and pepper. Cook, uncovered, over medium-low heat about 15 minutes or till liquid has evaporated and mixture is of spreading consistency, stirring occasionally.

Place the bread shell on a lightly greased baking sheet. Spread the warm tomato mixture over bread shell. Arrange the tomato slices and eggplant slices on the tomato mixture. Arrange zucchini slices and summer squash slices on top. Brush sliced vegetables with the remaining oil. Sprinkle with feta cheese and olives. Sprinkle with mozzarella cheese.

Bake in a 400° oven for 12 to 15 minutes or till cheese melts and vegetables are heated through. Makes 12 appetizer servings.

Nutrition information per serving: 162 calories, 6 g protein, 22 g carbohydrate, 6 g fat (1 g saturated), 7 mg cholesterol, 350 mg sodium, 205 mg potassium.

SMOKED SALMON AND CHÈVRE PIZZA

This trendsetting appetizer pizza offers an elegant start to a special occasion dinner.

4   ounces soft goat cheese (chèvre)
2   tablespoons dairy sour cream
2   teaspoons prepared horseradish
1   16-ounce package Boboli (12-inch
      Italian bread shell)
3   ounces thinly sliced smoked salmon
      (lox-style), cut into ½-inch strips
1   tablespoon snipped fresh dill or
      1 teaspoon dried dillweed

In a small mixing bowl combine goat cheese, sour cream, and horse-radish. Mix well.

Place the bread shell on a lightly greased baking sheet. Spread goat cheese mixture evenly over the bread shell. Arrange salmon over goat cheese mixture. Sprinkle with dill.

Bake in a 400° oven about 8 minutes or till heated through. Makes 12 appetizer servings.

Nutrition information per serving: 138 calories, 7 g protein, 17 g carbohydrate, 5 g fat (2 g saturated), 9 mg cholesterol, 299 mg sodium, 21 mg potassium.

PROVENÇAL PIZZA

A touch of American ingenuity—frozen bread dough—simplifies a country French version of an Italian pizza.

1   16-ounce loaf frozen bread dough, thawed
4   medium onions, thinly sliced and separated into rings (4 cups)
2   cloves garlic, minced
1   teaspoon dried basil, crushed
1   teaspoon dried oregano, crushed
½   teaspoon fennel seed, crushed
2   tablespoons cooking oil
4   ripe medium tomatoes, peeled, seeded, and chopped
1½ cups shredded mozzarella cheese (6 ounces)
½   of a red sweet pepper, cut into bite-size strips
½   of a yellow and/or green sweet pepper, cut into bite-size strips
1   2¼-ounce can sliced pitted ripe olives, drained

On a lightly floured surface, roll bread dough into a 16x12-inch rectangle. Transfer dough to a greased 15x10x1-inch baking pan. Prick generously with a fork. Let dough stand for 5 minutes. Bake in a 425° oven about 10 minutes or till light brown; cool crust.

Meanwhile, in a large skillet cook onions, garlic, basil, oregano, and fennel seed, uncovered, in hot oil over medium heat about 20 minutes or till onions are tender but not brown, stirring frequently. Stir in chopped tomatoes; cook, uncovered, for 10 minutes more, stirring frequently. Spread tomato mixture over cooled crust. Sprinkle with mozzarella cheese. Arrange sweet pepper strips atop cheese. Sprinkle with olives.

Bake for 12 to 15 minutes more or till cheese melts and pizza is heated through. Makes 20 appetizer servings.

Nutrition information per serving: 114 calories, 5 g protein, 15 g carbohydrate, 4 g fat (1 g saturated), 5 mg cholesterol, 74 mg sodium, 167 mg potassium.

FONTINA CHEESE AND ARTICHOKE PIZZA

Fontina is a firm, creamy, delicate-tasting Italian cheese. If you can't find it at your grocery store, Swiss cheese makes a good substitute.

1   medium red onion, thinly sliced
2   cloves garlic, minced
1   tablespoon olive oil or cooking oil
1   16-ounce package Boboli (12-inch
      Italian bread shell)
1½ cups shredded fontina or Swiss cheese
      (6 ounces)
1   9-ounce package frozen artichoke
      hearts, thawed
      Coarsely ground pepper

In a small skillet cook onion and garlic in hot oil till tender and golden brown; set aside.

Place the bread shell on a lightly greased baking sheet. Sprinkle with *½ cup* of the fontina or Swiss cheese. Top with onion mixture. Cut up artichoke hearts; arrange atop cheese. Sprinkle with remaining cheese. Sprinkle lightly with pepper.

Bake in a 450° oven for 8 to 10 minutes or till cheese melts and pizza is heated through. Makes 12 appetizer servings.

Nutrition information per serving: 179 calories, 9 g protein, 20 g carbohydrate, 8 g fat (0 g saturated), 18 mg cholesterol, 227 mg sodium, 88 mg potassium.

WHOLE WHEAT PIZZA TART

After baking the pizza crust until it's light brown, you can cool it completely and let it stand, covered, at room temperature until you're ready to finish the recipe.

1   16-ounce loaf frozen whole wheat bread dough, thawed
1   green onion or leek
¼   of a small yellow or green sweet pepper
¼   cup pizza sauce
¼   cup purchased pesto or Homemade Pesto (see recipe, page 119)
1½ cups shredded provolone or mozzarella cheese (6 ounces)
    Assorted toppings such as thinly sliced tomatoes, sliced fresh mushrooms, sliced eggplant, sliced pepperoni, and sliced pitted ripe olives

On a lightly floured surface, roll bread dough into a 11-inch circle. Transfer dough to an 11-inch tart pan with a removable bottom. Press dough into bottom and up sides of pan. Prick generously with a fork. Bake in a 400° oven for 12 to 15 minutes or till light brown.

Meanwhile, cut green onion or leek and sweet pepper into long, thin strips. In a medium saucepan, cook onion or leek and sweet pepper, covered, in a small amount of boiling water for 2 to 3 minutes or till tender; drain completely.

Spread pizza sauce over *half* of the hot crust; spread pesto over remaining *half* of crust. Sprinkle with provolone or mozzarella cheese. Arrange green onion or leek, sweet pepper, and other desired toppings atop cheese.

Bake for 10 to 15 minutes more or till cheese melts and pizza is heated through. Makes 10 to 12 appetizer servings.

Nutrition information per serving: 225 calories, 9 g protein, 24 g carbohydrate, 10 g fat (3 g saturated), 13 mg cholesterol, 250 mg sodium, 206 mg potassium.

SHRIMP AND SHIITAKE MUSHROOM PIZZA SQUARES

Shiitake (shih TOCK ee) mushrooms are brown, Oriental mushrooms with large, floppy caps. They have a rich, meaty flavor.

1   **16-ounce loaf frozen bread dough, thawed**
1   **egg white**
1   **tablespoon water**
¼   **cup toasted pine nuts or slivered almonds**
    Parmesan Pizza Sauce (see recipe, page 5)
1   **cup chopped fresh spinach**
½   **pound fresh or frozen peeled and deveined shrimp, cooked and halved lengthwise**
1   **cup sliced fresh shiitake or white mushrooms**
1   **cup shredded Swiss cheese (4 ounces)**

On a lightly floured surface, roll bread dough into a 14x10-inch rectangle. Transfer dough to a lightly greased large baking sheet. Build up edges slightly; score edges with a knife, if desired. Prick generously with a fork. Combine egg white and water; brush over dough. Bake in a 375° oven for 20 to 25 minutes or till light brown.

Stir pine nuts or almonds into Parmesan Pizza Sauce; spread over hot crust. Top with spinach, shrimp, and mushrooms. Sprinkle with Swiss cheese.

Bake about 12 minutes more or till cheese melts and pizza is heated through. Makes 12 appetizer servings.

Nutrition information per serving: 194 calories, 12 g protein, 19 g carbohydrate, 6 g fat (3 g saturated), 41 mg cholesterol, 145 mg sodium, 154 mg potassium.

GARLIC, BRIE, AND PESTO MINI-PIZZAS

Cooking the garlic slowly over medium-low heat brings out a mellow, almost sweet flavor.

2   whole heads garlic
¼   cup olive oil or cooking oil
1   10-ounce package refrigerated pizza
     dough
½   cup purchased pesto or Homemade
     Pesto (see recipe, page 119)
8   ounces cold Brie or Camembert
     cheese, cut into ⅛-inch-thick slices

Place whole heads of garlic in a small heavy saucepan with oil. Cook and stir over medium-low heat for 5 minutes. Cover and reduce heat to low for 15 minutes or till garlic is tender. Remove heads of garlic from oil; drain on paper towels. Cool.

Unroll pizza dough. Roll or stretch dough into a 15x10-inch rectangle; cut into six 5-inch squares. Transfer squares to a lightly greased 15x10x1-inch baking pan. Prick generously with a fork. Bake in a 425° oven for 7 to 8 minutes or till lightly browned.

Spread pesto over hot crusts. Arrange Brie or Camembert cheese slices atop pesto. Divide heads of garlic into cloves and peel. With a small, sharp knife, cut cloves lengthwise in half (small cloves can be left whole). Press garlic pieces into cheese. Bake pizzas for 8 to 10 minutes more or till cheese softens. To serve, cut each pizza square in half diagonally. Makes 12 appetizer servings.

Nutrition information per serving: 243 calories, 8 g protein, 14 g carbohydrate, 17 g fat (1 g saturated), 20 mg cholesterol, 310 mg sodium, 33 mg potassium.

ITALIAN VEGETABLE PIZZAS

Asiago (ah see AH go) cheese is a hard cheese with a sharp flavor. Look for it in large supermarkets or specialty shops.

2   tablespoons clear Italian salad dressing
½   pound asparagus, cut into 2-inch pieces, or one 10-ounce package frozen cut asparagus, thawed
1   medium yellow summer squash or zucchini, cut into julienne strips (1½ cups)
1   cup sliced fresh mushrooms
3   8-ounce packages Boboli (six 6-inch Italian bread shells)
¼   cup clear Italian salad dressing
1   ripe large tomato, seeded and chopped (1 cup)
¼   teaspoon coarsely ground pepper
1   cup shredded mozzarella cheese (4 ounces)
⅓   cup finely shredded asiago or Parmesan cheese

In a medium skillet heat the 2 tablespoons Italian salad dressing. Add asparagus and summer squash or zucchini; cook and stir for 2 minutes. Add mushrooms; cook and stir 1 minute more.

Place bread shells on a lightly greased baking sheet. Brush bread shells with the ¼ cup Italian salad dressing. Using a slotted spoon, top bread shells with the cooked asparagus mixture. Top with chopped tomato; sprinkle with pepper. Combine mozzarella cheese and asiago or Parmesan cheese; sprinkle over pizzas.

Bake in a 400° oven about 8 minutes or till cheese melts and pizzas are heated through. Cut the pizzas into wedges to serve. Makes 12 appetizer servings.

Nutrition information per serving: 249 calories, 11 g protein, 27 g carbohydrate, 12 g fat (2 g saturated), 10 mg cholesterol, 427 mg sodium, 137 mg potassium.

WALNUT AND CARAMELIZED ONION APPETIZER PIZZA

Serve this rich-tasting pizza as an hors d'oeuvre with glasses of a robust red wine.

2 tablespoons margarine or butter
4 medium onions, thinly sliced
   (about 4 cups)
2 teaspoons sugar
1 10-ounce package refrigerated pizza
   dough
1 5-ounce container semi-soft cheese
   with garlic and herbs
½ cup walnut pieces

In a large saucepan melt margarine or butter. Add onions. Cover and cook over medium-low heat about 15 minutes or till onions are tender and golden, stirring occasionally. Sprinkle sugar over onions. Cook, uncovered, for 10 to 15 minutes more or till browned, stirring occasionally.

Meanwhile, lightly grease an 11- to 13-inch pizza pan. Unroll pizza dough and transfer to greased pan, pressing dough out with your hands. Build up edges slightly. Prick generously with a fork. Bake in a 425° oven for 7 to 10 minutes or till lightly browned.

Spread cheese evenly over hot crust. Top with onions and walnut pieces. Bake for 10 to 12 minutes more or till heated through. Makes 12 appetizer servings.

Nutrition information per serving: 161 calories, 3 g protein, 15 g carbohydrate, 10 g fat (3 g saturated), 10 mg cholesterol, 166 mg sodium, 145 mg potassium.

POLISH PIZZA

Serve this potato-filled bread on its own as an appetizer or with a hearty soup for dinner.

¼   cup warm water (105° to 115°)
1   package active dry yeast
1   teaspoon sugar
2½ to 3 cups all-purpose flour
2   tablespoons sugar
½   teaspoon salt
1   slightly beaten egg
½   cup milk
2   tablespoons margarine or butter, melted
2   tablespoons cooking oil
2   medium potatoes, peeled and cut up
½   cup shredded sharp cheddar cheese (2 ounces)
2   tablespoons margarine or butter
¼   teaspoon salt
1   tablespoon margarine or butter, melted

For dough, combine warm water, yeast, and the 1 teaspoon sugar; stir to dissolve yeast. Set aside. In a large bowl mix *1½ cups* of the flour, 2 tablespoons sugar, and the ½ teaspoon salt. Make a well in the center; stir in egg. Heat milk to 120° to 130°; stir into flour mixture. Stir in 2 tablespoons melted margarine and the oil. Stir in yeast mixture. Using a spoon, stir in as much of the remaining flour as you can.

Turn out onto a floured surface. Knead in enough remaining flour to make a moderately stiff dough that is smooth and elastic (6 to 8 minutes total). Shape into a ball. Place in a greased bowl; turn dough once. Cover; let rise in a warm place till double (about 1 hour).

Meanwhile, for filling, place potatoes in a medium saucepan; add water to cover. Sprinkle with a little salt. Bring to boiling. Reduce heat and simmer, covered, for 20 to 25 minutes or till tender; drain. Add cheddar cheese, 2 tablespoons margarine or butter, and the ¼ teaspoon salt; mash till smooth. Set aside.

Punch dough down. Turn out onto a lightly floured surface. Divide dough in half. Cover and let rest 10 minutes. On a lightly floured surface, roll one portion of dough into a 15x12-inch rectangle. Transfer rectangle to a lightly greased baking sheet. Spread filling over dough to within 1 inch of edges. Roll remaining dough to a 15x12-inch rectangle; place over filling. Pinch edges to seal. Prick dough every 2 inches to allow steam to escape.

Bake in a 400° oven about 20 minutes or till golden brown, covering with foil the last 5 minutes. Brush with 1 tablespoon melted margarine. Serve warm or cool. Makes 24 to 30 appetizer servings.

Nutrition information per serving: 106 calories, 3 g protein, 13 g carbohydrate, 5 g fat (1 g saturated), 12 mg cholesterol, 115 mg sodium, 71 mg potassium.

PASTRAMI PIZZA BITES

A tasty combination of spicy pastrami, ripe olives, mozzarella cheese, and alfalfa sprouts make this easy French bread pizza a winner.

¼ cup margarine or butter, melted
½ teaspoon dried basil, crushed
¼ teaspoon dried oregano, crushed
⅛ teaspoon pepper
1 16-inch loaf French bread, split lengthwise
8 ounces sliced pastrami
1 6-ounce can tomato paste
⅓ cup chili sauce
¼ cup chopped green pepper
¼ cup chopped pitted ripe olives
2 tablespoons sliced green onion
1½ cups shredded mozzarella cheese (6 ounces)
1 medium tomato, chopped
¼ cup grated Parmesan cheese
1 cup alfalfa sprouts

In a small mixing bowl stir together melted margarine or butter, basil, oregano, and pepper; brush over cut sides of bread loaf halves.

Place both bread loaf halves, buttered side up, on a large baking sheet. Top with pastrami slices. In a small bowl stir together tomato paste, chili sauce, green pepper, olives, and green onion; spread over pastrami slices.

Bake in a 400° oven for 15 minutes. Sprinkle with mozzarella cheese, chopped tomato, and Parmesan cheese. Bake for 3 to 5 minutes more or till mozzarella cheese melts and pizza is heated through. Top with alfalfa sprouts. Slice each bread loaf half into 8 pieces. Makes 16 appetizer servings.

Nutrition information per serving: 175 calories, 10 g protein, 20 g carbohydrate, 6 g fat (2 g saturated), 20 mg cholesterol, 511 mg sodium, 253 mg potassium.

FOUR-CHEESE PIZZA

For a tasty pasta side dish on another night, toss the leftover Homemade Pesto with hot cooked fettuccine or or other pasta.

1 **10-ounce package refrigerated pizza dough**
   Homemade Pesto or ⅓ cup purchased pesto
½ **cup shredded cheddar cheese (2 ounces)**
½ **cup shredded mozzarella cheese (2 ounces)**
½ **cup shredded fontina cheese (2 ounces)**
½ **cup semi-soft goat cheese (chèvre), cut into small cubes**

Lightly grease an 11- to 13-inch pizza pan. Unroll pizza dough and transfer to greased pan, pressing out dough with your hands. Build up edges slightly. Prick generously with a fork. Bake in a 425° oven for 7 to 10 minutes or till lightly browned.

Spread *half* of the Homemade Pesto or the ⅓ cup purchased pesto over hot crust. (Reserve remaining Homemade Pesto for another use.) Sprinkle cheddar cheese over *one-fourth* of the pizza crust. Sprinkle mozzarella cheese over another *one-fourth* of the pizza crust. Sprinkle fontina cheese over another *one-fourth* of the pizza crust. Sprinkle chèvre over remaining *one-fourth* of the crust. Bake about 12 minutes more or till cheese melts. Makes 24 appetizer servings.

Homemade Pesto: In a blender container or food processor bowl combine 1 cup firmly packed *fresh basil leaves;* ½ cup firmly packed *parsley sprigs* (stems removed); ½ cup grated *Parmesan or Romano cheese;* ¼ cup pine *nuts, walnuts, or almonds;* ¼ teaspoon *salt;* and 1 large clove *garlic,* minced. Cover and blend or process with several on-off turns till a paste forms, stopping the machine several times and scraping the sides. With the machine running slowly, gradually add ¼ cup *olive oil or cooking oil* and blend or process till the consistency of soft butter.
Note: The pesto recipe makes enough for two pizzas. Freeze the remaining Homemade Pesto for up to 1 month or refrigerate for up to 2 days.

Nutrition information per serving: 79 calories, 3 g protein, 5 g carbohydrate, 5 g fat (1 g saturated), 8 mg cholesterol, 98 mg sodium, 14 mg potassium.

MEDITERRANEAN APPETIZER PIZZA

For a light supper for four, pair this distinctive pizza with a tossed green salad and dry white wine.

1 large sweet onion, thinly sliced and
   separated into rings
1 large yellow or red sweet pepper, cut
   into thin bite-size strips
2 tablespoons olive oil or cooking oil
1 16-ounce package Boboli (12-inch
   Italian bread shell)
1 4½-ounce can chopped ripe olives,
   drained
4 ounces semi-soft goat cheese (chèvre),
   cut into small pieces
2 tablespoons toasted pine nuts or
   toasted chopped walnuts
1 tablespoon snipped fresh oregano or
   1 teaspoon dried oregano, crushed
   Small fresh oregano leaves (optional)

In a large skillet cook onion and yellow or red sweet pepper in hot oil till very tender. Set aside.

Place the bread shell on a lightly greased baking sheet. Sprinkle ripe olives over bread shell. Top with onion mixture. Sprinkle with goat cheese, pine nuts or walnuts, and snipped oregano. Bake in a 400° oven about 8 minutes or till heated through. If desired, top with whole oregano leaves. Makes 12 appetizer servings.

Nutrition information per serving: 187 calories, 7 g protein, 19 g carbohydrate, 11 g fat (2 g saturated), 10 mg cholesterol, 330 mg sodium, 69 mg potassium.

STRAWBERRY-MASCARPONE DESSERT PIZZA

Mascarpone cheese looks and tastes like cream cheese except it's richer. Look for it at supermarkets, cheese shops, and Italian specialty stores.

1⅓ cups all-purpose flour
⅓ cup packed brown sugar
⅔ cup margarine or butter, softened
⅔ cup whipping cream
8 ounces mascarpone cheese or soft-style cream cheese
¾ cup sifted powdered sugar
½ teaspoon finely shredded lemon peel
4 cups sliced strawberries
   Chocolate curls or grated chocolate (optional)

For crust, in a medium mixing bowl combine flour and brown sugar. Cut in margarine or butter till mixture resembles coarse crumbs. Press firmly into an 11- to 13-inch pizza pan. Bake in a 400° oven for 10 to 15 minutes or till light brown. Cool completely.

Just before serving, in a medium mixing bowl beat whipping cream with an electric mixer on low speed just till soft peaks form. Add mascarpone cheese or cream cheese, powdered sugar, and lemon peel; beat till fluffy (mixture will thicken as it is beaten).

Spread cheese mixture atop cooled crust. Top with strawberries. Garnish with chocolate curls or grated chocolate, if desired. Serve immediately. Makes 12 servings.

Nutrition information per serving: 329 calories, 6 g protein, 27 g carbohydrate, 24 g fat (10 g saturated), 42 mg cholesterol, 138 mg sodium, 133 mg potassium.

ROCKY ROAD COOKIE PIZZA

This yummy dessert pizza reminded our Taste Panel of a great big chocolate chip cookie topped with marshmallows, peanuts, and caramel topping.

¾ cup margarine or butter
1¾ cups all-purpose flour
½ cup granulated sugar
½ cup packed brown sugar
1 egg
1 teaspoon vanilla
1 cup tiny marshmallows
1 cup miniature semisweet chocolate
  pieces
½ cup chopped peanuts
⅓ cup caramel ice cream topping

Lightly grease a 13-inch pizza pan. For crust, in a large mixing bowl beat margarine or butter with an electric mixer on medium to high speed for 30 seconds. Add about *half* of the flour, the granulated sugar, brown sugar, egg, and vanilla. Beat mixture till thoroughly combined. Beat in remaining flour.

Spread dough evenly into prepared pizza pan. Bake in a 350° oven for 25 to 27 minutes or till edges are golden brown and center is set. Remove from oven. Sprinkle evenly with marshmallows, chocolate pieces, and peanuts. Drizzle with caramel ice cream topping.

Bake about 5 minutes more or till marshmallows are golden. Cool on a wire rack. Makes 12 servings.

Nutrition information per serving: 371 calories, 10 g protein, 50 g carbohydrate, 19 g fat (3 g saturated), 18 mg cholesterol, 202 mg sodium, 148 mg potassium.

PEACH-PECAN PIZZA

In the winter months when fresh peaches are hard to find, top this pizza with 2 cups thinly sliced bananas.

1¾ cups all-purpose flour
¼ teaspoon salt
½ cup shortening
⅓ cup finely chopped pecans
4 to 5 tablespoons cold water
¾ cup sugar
¼ cup cornstarch or ½ cup all-purpose flour
3 cups milk
4 beaten egg yolks
1 tablespoon margarine or butter
1 teaspoon vanilla
½ cup peach or apricot preserves
2 cups thinly sliced, peeled fresh peaches
¼ cup toasted coarsely chopped pecans or toasted flaked coconut

For crust, in a medium mixing bowl combine flour and salt. Cut in shortening till pieces are the size of small peas. Stir in the ⅓ cup pecans. Sprinkle *1 tablespoon* of the water over part of flour mixture, gently tossing with a fork. Push to the side of the bowl. Repeat with remaining water till all is moistened. Form dough into a ball. On a lightly floured surface, flatten dough with hands. Roll dough from center to edges, forming a circle about 15 inches in diameter.

Fold pastry into quarters and transfer to a 12- or 13-inch pizza pan. Unfold pastry and ease into pan. Trim pastry to ½ inch beyond edge of pan. Fold under pastry and flute edge. Prick pastry with a fork. Bake in a 425° oven for 12 to 15 minutes or till golden. Cool.

Meanwhile, for filling, in a heavy medium saucepan stir together sugar and cornstarch or flour. Gradually stir in milk. Cook and stir over medium heat till thickened and bubbly. Cook and stir 2 minutes more. Remove from heat.

Gradually stir about *1 cup* of the hot mixture into egg yolks. Return all egg yolk mixture to saucepan. Cook and stir till mixture begins to bubble. Reduce heat. Cook and stir for 2 minutes more. Remove from heat. Stir in margarine or butter and vanilla. Cover surface with plastic wrap. Cool to room temperature. (*Do not* stir.)

Spread peach or apricot preserves on cooled pastry. Spread filling on top of preserves. Cover with plastic wrap. Chill for 4 to 24 hours. Just before serving, arrange peach slices on top of filling. Sprinkle with the ¼ cup pecans or coconut. Makes 16 servings.

Nutrition information per serving: 253 calories, 4 g protein, 33 g carbohydrate, 12 g fat (3 g saturated), 57 mg cholesterol, 68 mg sodium, 155 mg potassium.

CANDY-BAR PIZZA SUNDAES

Try strawberry, coffee, or your personal favorite flavor of ice cream on these decadent brownie pizza wedges.

1   21½-ounce package fudge brownie
    mix
½   cup water
¼   cup cooking oil
1   egg
1   quart chocolate ice cream
    White Chocolate Sauce
2   cups cut-up candy bars (chocolate-
    coated caramel-topped nougat bars,
    chocolate-covered English toffee,
    chocolate-covered peanut butter
    cups, and/or white chocolate candy
    bars)
¼   cup chopped nuts (optional)
    Sliced fresh strawberries (optional)

In a large mixing bowl combine brownie mix, water, oil, and egg. Stir till well combined. Spread dough evenly into a greased 12-inch pizza pan with ½-inch sides. Bake in a 375° oven for 18 to 20 minutes. Cool completely.

Cut crust into 12 wedges; do not remove from pan. Place small scoops of chocolate ice cream on each wedge. Cover tightly and freeze till firm.

Just before serving, pour warm White Chocolate Sauce over ice cream. Sprinkle with cut-up candy bars. If desired, sprinkle with chopped nuts and garnish with fresh strawberries. Serve immediately. Makes 12 servings.

White Chocolate Sauce: In a heavy medium saucepan bring ⅔ cup *whipping cream* and 1 teaspoon *vanilla* just to boiling, stirring frequently. Remove saucepan from heat. In a small mixing bowl beat 1 *egg yolk,* ⅓ cup *sugar,* and 2 to 4 tablespoons of the hot whipping cream mixture with an electric mixer on medium speed for 2 to 3 minutes or till thick and lemon-colored. Gradually stir about half of the remaining whipping cream mixture into the egg yolk mixture. Return all to the saucepan. Cook and stir over medium heat just till mixture returns to boiling. Remove from heat. Stir in 2 ounces (½ cup) grated *white baking bar.* Continue stirring till bar melts. Cover surface with plastic wrap; cool for 15 minutes. Stir before serving. Store any remaining sauce in the refrigerator.

Nutrition information per serving: 483 calories, 5 g protein, 72 g carbohydrate, 21 g fat (10 g saturated), 62 mg cholesterol, 259 mg sodium, 278 mg potassium.

FRUIT PIZZA WITH PINEAPPLE GLAZE

With its cream cheese and fruit topping, this pizza will remind you of a cheesecake.

1¾ cups all-purpose flour
¼ teaspoon salt
½ cup shortening
4 to 5 tablespoons cold water
3 tablespoons granulated sugar
1 tablespoon cornstarch
1 cup unsweetened pineapple juice
1 8-ounce container soft-style cream
    cheese with pineapple
¾ cup sifted powdered sugar
3 cups assorted fresh fruit such as
    peeled and sliced pineapple; sliced
    kiwi fruit, plums, or nectarines;
    halved strawberries; and/or whole
    raspberries or blueberries

For crust, in a medium mixing bowl combine flour and salt. Cut in shortening till pieces are the size of small peas. Sprinkle *1 tablespoon* water over part of flour mixture, gently tossing with a fork. Push to the side of the bowl. Repeat with remaining water till all is moistened. Form dough into a ball. On a lightly floured surface, flatten dough with hands. Roll from center to edges, forming a circle about 15-inches in diameter.

Fold pastry into quarters and transfer to a 13-inch pizza pan. Unfold pastry and ease into pan. Trim pastry to ½ inch beyond edge of pan. Fold under extra pastry and flute edge. Prick pastry with a fork. Bake in a 425° oven for 12 to 15 minutes or till golden. Cool.

Meanwhile, for glaze, in a small saucepan combine granulated sugar and cornstarch. Stir in pineapple juice. Cook and stir till thickened and bubbly. Cook and stir 2 minutes more. Cover surface of mixture with plastic wrap; cool.

In a small mixing bowl combine cream cheese and powdered sugar. Beat till well mixed. To assemble pizza, spread the cream cheese mixture over cooled pastry. Arrange fruit on top of cream cheese mixture. Carefully spoon cooled glaze over fruit. Chill for up to 2 hours before serving. Makes 16 servings.

Nutrition information per serving: 204 calories, 2 g protein, 26 g carbohydrate, 11 g fat (4 g saturated), 12 mg cholesterol, 79 mg sodium, 136 mg potassium.

BERRY-BANANA BROWNIE PIZZA

To melt either the unsweetened or semisweet chocolate in your microwave oven, place it and the margarine, butter, or shortening in a microwave-safe custard cup or measure. Micro-cook, uncovered, on 100% power (high) for 1 to 2 minutes, stirring after 1 minute.

1   cup margarine or butter
4   ounces unsweetened chocolate
2   cups sugar
4   eggs
1   teaspoon vanilla
1½   cups all-purpose flour
2   3-ounce packages cream cheese, softened
¼   cup sugar
1   egg
½   teaspoon vanilla
2   bananas, sliced
2   cups sliced strawberries
1   ounce semisweet chocolate
½   teaspoon shortening

In a medium saucepan melt margarine or butter and unsweetened chocolate over low heat. Remove from heat. Stir in the 2 cups sugar, the 4 eggs, and the 1 teaspoon vanilla. Beat lightly by hand just till combined. Stir in flour.

Spread batter in a lightly greased 12-inch pizza pan with ¾-inch sides. Bake in a 350° oven about 20 minutes or till just set in center.

Meanwhile, beat cream cheese, the ¼ cup sugar, the 1 egg, and the ½ teaspoon vanilla till combined. Spread cream cheese mixture over hot brownie crust. Bake for 8 to 10 minutes more or till cream cheese mixture is set. Cover and chill for up to 24 hours.

Just before serving, arrange sliced bananas and sliced strawberries over cream cheese mixture. In a small heavy saucepan heat semisweet chocolate and shortening over low heat till melted; drizzle over fruit. Makes 12 to 16 servings.

Nutrition information per serving: 491 calories, 7 g protein, 59 g carbohydrate, 28 g fat (9 g saturated), 104 mg cholesterol, 250 mg sodium, 276 mg potassium.

BERRY-RICOTTA PIZZA

This fresh fruit dessert pizza can be partially assembled several hours before serving. Spread the ricotta mixture over the baked and cooled crust and chill for 3 to 4 hours. Then just before serving, top with your choice of fresh berries.

1   16-ounce loaf frozen sweet bread
      dough, thawed
1   cup ricotta cheese
3   tablespoons sugar
½   teaspoon vanilla
½   teaspoon finely shredded lemon or
      orange peel
2   to 3 cups red raspberries, blackberries,
      blueberries, and/or sliced
      strawberries
1   tablespoon powdered sugar

Press bread dough into a greased 13-inch pizza pan. Prick generously with a fork. Bake in a 375° oven for 20 to 25 minutes or till light brown. Cool crust completely on a wire rack.

Meanwhile, for filling, in a small mixing bowl stir together ricotta cheese, sugar, vanilla, and lemon or orange peel.

Spread filling over crust. Top with desired berries. Sift powdered sugar over berries. Makes 12 servings.

Nutrition information per serving: 145 calories, 5 g protein, 25 g carbohydrate, 3 g fat (1 g saturated), 6 mg cholesterol, 151 mg sodium, 137 mg potassium.

EASTER COOKIE PIZZA
Celebrate the holidays throughout the year with this festive dessert.

1 20-ounce roll refrigerated sugar cookie dough, cut into ¼-inch-thick slices
1 6-ounce package (1 cup) semisweet chocolate pieces
½ cup creamy peanut butter
1½ cups jelly beans, small gumdrops, or chopped pastel cream mint kisses
2 tablespoons flaked coconut

Press cookie dough slices into a greased 13-inch pizza pan. Bake in a 350° oven 15 to 20 minutes or till golden. Immediately sprinkle with chocolate pieces; drop peanut butter by spoonfuls atop chocolate pieces. Let stand 5 minutes. Gently spread chocolate and peanut butter over crust. Sprinkle with candy and coconut. Makes 12 servings.

Nutrition information per serving: 392 calories, 6 g protein, 58 g carbohydrate, 19 g fat (4 g saturated), 15 mg cholesterol, 262 mg sodium, 135 mg potassium.

Halloween Cookie Pizza: Prepare as directed except omit jelly beans and coconut. Sprinkle 1 cup *candy corn or candy-coated peanut butter-flavored pieces* and ½ cup *raisins* over chocolate mixture.

Nutrition information per serving: 433 calories, 7 g protein, 52 g carbohydrate, 23 g fat (8 g saturated), 17 mg cholesterol, 260 mg sodium, 178 mg potassium.

Christmas Cookie Pizza: Prepare as directed except omit jelly beans and coconut. Sprinkle 1½ cups *red and green candy-coated milk chocolate pieces* over chocolate mixture.

Nutrition information per serving: 443 calories, 8 g protein, 53 g carbohydrate, 23 g fat (4 g saturated), 15 mg cholesterol, 260 mg sodium, 133 mg potassium.

Valentine Cookie Pizza: Prepare as directed except omit jelly beans and coconut. Sprinkle 1½ cups *red and white candy-coated milk chocolate pieces* over chocolate mixture.

Nutrition information per serving: 443 calories, 8 g protein, 53 g carbohydrate, 23 g fat (4 g saturated), 15 mg cholesterol, 260 mg sodium, 133 mg potassium.

EASY APPLE PIE CALZONE

Serve this fruit-filled calzone just like you would a slice of apple pie—with a scoop of vanilla ice cream.

½ of a 15-ounce package (1 crust) folded
   refrigerated unbaked piecrust
1½ cups thinly sliced, peeled cooking
   apples
3 tablespoons water
1 teaspoon lemon juice
¼ cup packed brown sugar
1 tablespoon all-purpose flour
¼ teaspoon ground cinnamon
   Dash ground allspice
1 tablespoon margarine or butter
1 teaspoon milk
1 teaspoon granulated sugar

Let piecrust stand at room temperature according to package directions.

Meanwhile, in a medium saucepan combine apples, water, and lemon juice. Bring just to boiling. Reduce heat. Cover and simmer about 5 minutes or till apples are tender. Combine the brown sugar, flour, cinnamon, and allspice; stir into apple mixture. Cook and stir till thickened and bubbly. Remove from heat; stir in margarine or butter. Cool for 15 to 20 minutes.

Unfold pie crust. Place on a lightly greased baking sheet. Spoon apple mixture evenly over *half* of crust to within ½ inch of edge. Moisten edges of dough with water. Fold dough in half over filling. Seal by pressing with tines of a fork. Flute edges, if desired. Cut slits in top. Brush with milk; sprinkle with the granulated sugar.

Bake in a 375° oven for 25 to 30 minutes or till golden. Serve warm or cool. Cut into wedges to serve. Makes 3 to 5 servings.

Nutrition information per serving: 468 calories, 3 g protein, 61 g carbohydrate, 24 g fat (1 g saturated), 20 mg cholesterol, 332 mg sodium, 164 mg potassium.

PIZZA PAN COOKIE WEDGES WITH FUDGY FROSTING

With a thick and chewy cookie crust, this dessert pizza makes a grand finale to any meal.

2   3-ounce packages cream cheese, softened
⅓   cup margarine or butter
¼   cup shortening
½   cup packed brown sugar
1   egg
½   teaspoon vanilla
1½   cups all-purpose flour
½   teaspoon baking soda
1   cup coarsely chopped semisweet chocolate
    Fudgy Frosting
¼   cup chopped lightly salted mixed nuts or peanuts

In a medium mixing bowl beat cream cheese, margarine or butter, and shortening with an electric mixer on medium to high speed for 30 seconds. Add brown sugar, egg, and vanilla. Beat till thoroughly combined. Beat in flour and baking soda on low speed just till combined. Stir in the chopped chocolate.

Spread cookie dough evenly in a greased 12- or 13-inch pizza pan. Bake in a 350° oven for 20 to 22 minutes or till lightly browned around the edges. Cool completely. Frost with Fudgy Frosting. Sprinkle with chopped nuts. Cut into wedges. Makes 12 servings.

Fudgy Frosting: In a small mixing bowl combine 2⅓ cups sifted *powdered sugar,* ¼ cup *unsweetened cocoa powder,* ¼ cup softened *margarine or butter,* 2 tablespoons *boiling water,* and ½ teaspoon *vanilla.* Beat with an electric mixer on low to medium speed till combined. Beat on medium speed about 1 minute more or till fluffy.

Nutrition information per serving: 431 calories, 5 g protein, 52 g carbohydrate, 24 g fat (6 g saturated), 33 mg cholesterol, 214 mg sodium, 165 mg potassium.

Keep track of your daily nutrition needs by using the information we provide at the end of each recipe. We've analyzed the nutritional content of each recipe serving for you. When a recipe gives an ingredient substitution, we used the first choice in the analysis. If it makes a range of servings (such as 4 to 6), we used the smallest number. Ingredients listed as optional weren't included in the calculations.

METRIC COOKING HINTS

By making a few conversions, cooks in Australia, Canada, and the United Kingdom can use the recipes in Better Homes and Gardens® *Pizzas* with confidence. The charts on this page provide a guide for converting measurements from the U.S. customary system, which is used throughout this book, to the imperial and metric systems. There also is a conversion table for oven temperatures to accommodate the differences in oven calibrations.

Volume and Weight: Americans traditionally use cup measures for liquid and solid ingredients. The chart (top right) shows the approximate imperial and metric equivalents. If you are accustomed to weighing solid ingredients, here are some helpful approximate equivalents.
- 1 cup butter, caster sugar, or rice = 8 ounces = about 250 grams
- 1 cup flour = 4 ounces = about 125 grams
- 1 cup icing sugar = 5 ounces = about 150 grams

Spoon measures are used for smaller amounts of ingredients although the size of the table-spoon varies slightly among countries, for practical purposes and for recipes in this book, a straight substitution is all that's necessary.

Measurements made using cups or spoons should always be level, unless stated otherwise.

Product Differences: Most of the ingredients called for in the recipes in this book are available in English-speaking countries. However, some are known by different names. Here are some common American ingredients and their possible counterparts:
- Sugar is granulated or caster sugar.
- Powdered sugar is icing sugar.
- All-purpose flour is plain household flour or white flour. When self-rising flour is used in place of all-purpose flour in a recipe that calls for leavening, omit the leavening agent (baking soda or baking powder) and salt.
- Light corn syrup is golden syrup.
- Cornstarch is cornflour.
- Baking soda is bicarbonate of soda.
- Vanilla is vanilla essence.

USEFUL EQUIVALENTS

⅛ teaspoon = 0.5 ml
¼ teaspoon = 1 ml
½ teaspoon = 2 ml
1 teaspoon = 5 ml
¼ cup = 2 fluid ounces = 50 ml
⅓ cup = 3 fluid ounces = 75 ml
½ cup = 4 fluid ounces = 125 ml

⅔ cup = 5 fluid ounces = 150 ml
¾ cup = 6 fluid ounces = 175 ml
1 cup = 8 fluid ounces = 250 ml
2 cups = 1 pint
2 pints = 1 litre
½ inch = 1 centimetre
1 inch = 2 centimetres

BAKING PAN SIZES

American	Metric
8x1½-inch round baking pan	20x4-centimetre sandwich or cake tin
9x1½-inch round baking pan	23x3.5-centimetre sandwich or cake tin
11x7x1½-inch baking pan	28x18x4-centimetre baking pan
13x9x2-inch baking pan	32.5x23x5-centimetre baking pan
2-quart rectangular baking dish	30x19x5-centimetre baking pan
15x10x1-inch baking pan	38x25.5x2.5-centimetre baking pan (Swiss roll tin)
9-inch pie plate	22x4- or 23x4-centimetre pie plate
7- or 8-inch springform pan	18- or 20-centimetre springform or loose-bottom cake tin
9x5x3-inch loaf pan	23x13x6-centimetre or 2-pound narrow loaf pan or paté tin
1½-quart casserole	1.5-litre casserole
2-quart casserole	2-litre casserole

OVEN TEMPERATURE EQUIVALENTS

Fahrenheit Setting	Celsius Setting*	Gas Setting
300°F	150°C	Gas Mark 2
325°F	160°C	Gas Mark 3
350°F	180°C	Gas Mark 4
375°F	190°C	Gas Mark 5
400°F	200°C	Gas Mark 6
425°F	220°C	Gas Mark 7
450°F	230°C	Gas Mark 8
Broil		Grill

*Electric and gas ovens may be calibrated using Celsius. However, increase the Celsius setting 10 to 20 degrees when cooking above 160°C with an electric oven. For convection or forced-air ovens (gas or electric), lower the temperature setting 10°C when cooking at all heat levels.